THE BOOK OF
AMAZING FACTS
Volume 1

Copyright © 2002

All rights reserved.
Printed in the USA.

Amazing Facts, Inc.
P.O. Box 1058
Roseville, CA 95678-8058
www.amazingfacts.org

Edited by Anthony Lester
Cover Design & Illustrations by Haley Trimmer
Layout by Greg Solie - Altamont Graphics
Final Copy Proofing by Tarah Solie

All Bible verses are from the KJV unless otherwise noted.

ISBN 1-58019-150-9

THE BOOK OF AMAZING FACTS, Vol. 1

Contents

FOREWORD

People by nature are curious creatures. I should know; I'm one of them! Anything out of the ordinary has the potential to capture our attention and stimulate our thinking. Entertainment, from trivia games to magazines and books, is often based around our propensity to be captivated by the bizarre and drawn to the incredible.

Jesus used man's natural inquisitiveness as a tool for teaching, and so can you. This incredible *Book of Amazing Facts* and other interesting trivia can be more than just a stimulating read. It's an excellent resource for teachers, pastors, and lay evangelists to illustrate the principles of God's Word with fascinating, not-so-typical facts.

The first volume is largely the product of my spending hours reading through encyclopedias, nature books, and science journals. Still others came from watching the *History Channel,* surfing the Internet, and e-mails from good friends.

Many of these facts have been used during the *Bible Answers Live* radio program, and others can be found in *Inside Report* articles and booklets published through the years. We have done our best to ensure accuracy where possible, but in many cases, we have simply depended on the faithfulness of our sources. If you happen to spot an inaccuracy along the way, write to let us know. We'll make appropriate corrections in future editions.

For now, consider many of these facts a springboard to more in-depth study of God's amazing planet and the people, animals, plants, inventions, buildings and everything else that call it home.

Doug Batchelor

Contents:

MIGRATION

Scientists are still mystified by how animals know when it's time to migrate. And how do they unerringly find their way back to the same beach, stream or feeding ground they've not seen since birth?

Consider the green turtles that swim from their feeding grounds off the coast of Brazil to tiny Ascension Island about 3,000 miles away, which they may not have visited since they were hatched. After depositing their eggs, they swim back to Brazil. The Chinook salmon migrates farther than any other salmon, traveling up to 2,000 miles inland to spawn in the exact freshwater streams as did their ancestors.

The monarch butterfly is known for its extraordinarily long migrations, which it makes twice in its two-year life span. During the summer months, millions of monarchs can be found fluttering from Canada and the United States to their winter home in central Mexico—traveling in some cases more than 2,000 miles!

And an estimated 10 billion birds engage in migratory flights annually. One species of shrike wings its way 3,500 miles from Central Asia to the Equator of Africa. The longest flight made by a homing pigeon was in 1931 from Arras, France, to Saigon, Vietnam. To demonstrate that homing pigeons are not guided by landmarks, the feisty fowl was taken to France in a covered cage aboard a ship. When released, the pigeon flew straight as an arrow 7,200 miles over unfamiliar land to its home in only 24 days.

But the Arctic tern has the longest migration of any animal. Winging each year from their nesting grounds in the Arctic North to the Antarctic and back, terns make a round-trip journey of nearly 25,000 miles!

It seems God has also placed this inner drive to migrate in many of His other creatures, but only when He has established a place for them to go.

Exodus 15:13 "Thou in thy mercy hast led forth the people which thou hast redeemed: thou hast guided them in thy strength unto thy holy habitation."

AND DID YOU KNOW...

- **Pricey Pooches:** Cost of raising a medium-size dog to the age of eleven: $6,400.

- **Whale Milk Shakes:** A humpback whale's milk is 54 percent fat.

STATOCYST STONE

Shrimp lay near the bottom of the marine food chain. But these little creatures have a strange habit that can teach us some important lessons. As shrimp mature, they outgrow their skins and need to molt. But every time a shrimp molts, it does something bizarre. It places a tiny piece of sand on its own head.

This grain of sand is called a "statocyst stone." Without it, the shrimp has a difficult time knowing which way is up. The small tug of gravity from the sand particle helps the shrimp to know if it is right-side up or upside down. The sand grain is crucial for the shrimp to maintain its equilibrium when tossed by the surging seas.

A marine biologist learned about this when he replaced sand with metal filings in an aquarium. When the shrimp began to molt, they stuck a tiny piece of steel in their heads instead of the usual grain of sand. The biologist then placed a magnet at the top of the tank, and the shrimp flipped upside down. The pull of the magnet was stronger than the tug of gravity.

The scientist then took shrimp from the ocean and put it into the aquarium with a grain of sand on its head. This shrimp was the only one who swam right-side up! The other inverted shrimp were probably thinking, "Look at that fanatic swimming upside down!"

That's exactly what humans do if anyone doesn't follow the crowd. We quickly assume something's wrong with them. And in this constantly changing world, it's easy for Christians to find themselves going the opposite direction of popular trends. We need something dependable to help us maintain our spiritual equilibrium. What is our "statocyst stone?" It is God's Word, the Holy Bible!

Psalm 119:105 "Thy word is a lamp unto my feet, and a light unto my path."

BALD EAGLES

Among the most unusual of the great birds, bald eagles primarily eat fish and live up to 40 years in the wild. Furthermore, they are monogamous and remain faithful to their mate until death. But these amazing birds are especially renowned for their excellent eyesight.

Eagles have two foveae, or centers of focus, in the retina of each eye that allow them to see both forward and to the side at the same time. (Human retinas have only one.) Depending on which way the eagle looks, the lens of its eye focuses an image on one fovea or the other. The rear fovea is for forward, stereoscopic vision, and the other is for looking sideways. Both foveae are more densely lined with rods and cones than those of human eyes, giving them much greater resolving power.

They also have eyelids that close during sleep. For blinking, they have an inner eyelid called a nictitating membrane. Every three or four seconds, the nictitating membrane slides across the eye from front to back, wiping dirt and dust from the cornea. Because the membrane is translucent, the eagle can see even while the membrane covers the eye.

Eagles have color vision, and while their eyes are not as large as a human's, their sharpness is at least four times that of a person with perfect vision. While soaring, gliding, or flapping, they are capable of seeing fish in the water from several hundred feet above or identify a rabbit moving almost a mile away. An eagle flying in a fixed position at an altitude of 1,000 feet could spot prey as small as a mouse over an area of almost three square miles!

Psalm 11:4 *"The* LORD *is in his holy temple, the* LORD'*s throne is in heaven: his eyes behold, his eyelids try, the children of men."*

Psalm 33:18 *"Behold, the eye of the* LORD *is upon them that fear him, upon them that hope in his mercy; ... "*

AND DID YOU KNOW...

- **Snakes!** Maine has no poisonous snakes. Hawaii has only two snakes. One is a sea snake rarely seen in Hawaii waters. The other is a blind snake that lives like an earthworm.
- **Fowl Flight:** The longest recorded flight of a chicken is 13 seconds.

BALD EAGLES 2

Because of its grace, strength and sheer size, the bald eagle was chosen to symbolize the United States. Here are some feathery amazing facts:

Baby eagles (or eaglets) begin their lives high in a tree in a nest typically five feet in diameter. Eagles often use the same nest year after year so that over the years, some nests grow to as much as an enormous nine feet in diameter and weighing two tons! After making the first break in the shell, it can take an eaglet 12 to 48 hours to completely hatch out.

The parents provide well for their offspring, and the young birds grow rapidly—they add one pound every five days. But eventually, they must learn to fly and hunt for themselves.

The mother teaches her eaglets to fly by making the nest very uncomfortable. She rips up the soft padding to expose sharp sticks, bones, and rocks. Then she stops bringing food, but she'll frequently fly by the nest of hungry eaglets sporting fresh fish or rabbits to tempt them to fly. The little eaglets become so hungry and uncomfortable they are eventually compelled to leave the nest and commit themselves to the unknown world of air outside.

Tragically, it's also incredibly dangerous to be the American eagle, for approximately 40 percent of young eagles do not survive their first flight. In general, it's believed that only about 1 in 10 eagles survive to adulthood (five years old). Some of the primary

reasons are:
- Gun shot wounds by hunters that kill for feathers and talons to sell on the black market
- Electrocution from landing on power poles, when their large wings bridge two wires resulting in fatal burns or heart failure
- Lead poisoning from eating wounded ducks, rabbits, and other game that eluded the hunter but later died. Three little shot pellets can kill an eagle
- Ingestion of poison from eating carrion, like coyotes or rats, that were poisoned
- Collisions with vehicles
- Starvation where the food is scarce, largely due to competition with man.

It can be tough to be an eagle; in fact, they were once declared an endangered species. But they've since made a comeback. *Not only do nations today choose animals as their national mascots or symbols, Bible prophecies use different beasts to identify kingdoms' characteristics and their futures!*

AND DID YOU KNOW...

- **Bad Example:** At President Andrew Jackson's funeral in 1845 his pet parrot was removed for swearing.
- **Donkey Risks:** Donkeys kill more people annually than plane crashes.

EAGLES

An eagle knows when a storm is approaching long before it breaks. Once alerted, it will fly to a high spot and wait for the storm winds to come. When the storm hits, the bird sets its wings so that the wind will pick it up and lift it above the storm. While the storm rages below, the eagle is soaring above it. The eagle does not escape the storm, but rather uses it to lift it higher. It rises on the winds that bring the storm.

When the storms of life come upon us, we can rise above them by setting our minds on God. The storms do not have to overcome us. We can allow God's power to lift us above them.

Psalm 107:29 *"He maketh the storm a calm, so that the waves*

thereof are still."
    Isaiah 25:4 *"For thou hast been a strength to the poor, a strength to the needy in his distress, a refuge from the storm, a shadow from the heat, when the blast of the terrible ones is as a storm against the wall."*

AND DID YOU KNOW...

- **Fat Tongues:** Most Elephants weigh less then the tongue of the blue whale.

- **Give Credit Where Due:** A giraffe can go longer without water then a camel.

BUZZARD, BAT & BUMBLEBEE

If you put a buzzard in a 6-foot-by-8-foot pen that's entirely open at the top, the bird, despite its ability to fly, will be an absolute prisoner. Why? A buzzard always begins flight with a run of 10 to 12 feet. Without this runway, it will not even attempt to fly—but will remain a prisoner for life, waddling around in a small jail with an open top.

The common bat is a remarkably nimble night creature in the air, but it cannot take off from a level place. If it's placed on flat ground, all it can do is shuffle about, helplessly and painfully, until it reaches some slanted ground from which to launch itself.

And a bumblebee, if dropped into an open glass tumbler, will stay there until it dies! It never sees the means of escape at the top, but persists in trying to find some way out through the sides near the bottom. It will continue to seek until it completely destroys itself through exhaustion.

Many people are like the buzzard, the bat and the bumblebee. They are struggling about with all their problems and frustrations, not ever realizing that the answer for victory and freedom is right there "above" them.

Philippians 4: 6-7 *"Be careful [anxious] for nothing; but in every thing by prayer and supplication with thanksgiving let your requests be made known unto God. And the peace of God, which passeth all understanding, shall keep your hearts and minds through Christ Jesus."*

BATS

These nocturnal beasts can be found all over the world, from Canada to warm tropical climates. They are the only mammals that truly fly. (Flying squirrels can only glide short distances.) No, they're not flying rodents; instead, they belong to an entirely different group called Chiroptera, (kiy-ro˘p-ter-on), which is Greek for "hand wing." Their wings are actually extensions of their hands with a thin membrane between the fingers. Unlike most birds, bats are able to fly at relatively low speeds with extreme maneuverability. This is achieved by the bat's extraordinary ability to vary the shape and curvature of their wings and thus dramatically vary their aerodynamic lift. Bats have been clocked at 60 mph and observed at altitudes of more than two miles above ground.

Bats arc also the most numerous of any mammal species. With nearly 1,000 varieties, they account for almost a quarter of all mammal species! The smallest bat, called the Hog-Nosed Bat, is the size of a bumblebee and weighs less than a penny. The largest bat, the Flying Fox, has a wingspan of more than six feet.

During the day, bats sleep in caves, tree cavities and man-made structures. Nearly all bats sleep, or roost, hanging upside down by their hind feet. Wherever large numbers of bats roost, huge piles of bat droppings (guano) accumulate. In many countries, guano is collected and used as a high-quality fertilizer for crops. The nitrogen and phosphorus in bat guano is so potent, at one time it was extracted and used in the manufacture of explosives.

Bats have only one baby a year and may live as long as 20 years, living in colonies that might number from 20 to 20,000. Bats are considered nature's best bug control, consuming astonishing quantities of insects. One colony of Mexican free-tailed bats devours as much as 250 tons of insects in a single night! Not all bats eat insects. Some eat fruit, fish, frogs, lizards, nectar, and even blood! Nearly all bats feed from twilight of dusk to dawn.

And contrary to popular belief, bats are not blind. In fact, many bats have exceptionally good eyesight designed for low levels of light. To get around in the dark, many bats rely on a sophisticated form of sonar known as echolocation. With this detection, bats emit short pulses of high-frequency sounds that are usually well above the threshold of human hearing. The sound waves spread out in front of the bat, striking any objects in its flight path and bouncing back in the form of an echo. By using this God-given radar, bats are able to discern the direction, distance, speed, and in some instances, the size and density of the objects around them.

Did you know that the Bible teaches us that God has an invisible heavenly radar that records our every move?

Revelation 20:12 *"And I saw the dead, small and great, stand before God; and the books were opened: and another book was opened, which is the book of life: and the dead were judged out of those things which were written in the books, according to their works."*

OSTRICHES

Once flourishing throughout Africa, the majority of Ostriches live in protected reserves on the continent's east coast. Male African ostriches grow as high as 9 feet and can weigh a hefty 345 pounds— making them the tallest and heaviest of all living birds.

They also have extremely strong legs useful for self-defense that also enable them to reach top speeds of 40 mph. They can maintain this speed for 30 minutes, making them one of the fastest animals on two legs.

Ostriches live in family groups consisting of one cock and several hens. During breeding season, each hen lays between 2 and 11 creamy white eggs in a communal nest, which is a hollowed out crater in the ground about 10 feet across. Eventually, these nests may contain up to 50 eggs, but only about 20 can be successfully incubated. The eggs of the ostrich are the largest laid by any bird, measuring from 6 to 8 inches long and weighing between 2 to 4 lbs. The record is 5.1 lbs! An ostrich egg has the volume of about 24 chicken eggs, and though the shell is only 1.5 mm thick, it can hold the weight of a grown man.

The cock and the hens take turns incubating the eggs. The hens sit on them during the day and the male at night. After about 42 days, the eggs hatch. The chicks quickly learn to follow the long legs of the male who cares for them.

Ostriches can live between 50 to 70 years with a diet mainly of flowers, leaves, and seeds. These sturdy birds are well adapted to living in dry conditions and are able to survive a 25 percent loss of body weight due to dehydration. In fact, an ostrich has one of the most advanced immune systems known to mankind.

Unfortunately, they are not the smartest birds. In fact, an ostrich's eye is larger than its brain! Yet the notion that they bury their heads in the sand is actually a myth. Sadly, these tallest, fastest and biggest of birds also cannot fly, so they are easily farmed throughout the world for meat, feathers and leather.

The Bible teaches us that the greatest of the angels had his wings clipped because his eye was too big and his brain too small.

AND DID YOU KNOW...

- **Fowl Deal:** 90 percent of all species that have become extinct have been birds.

- **One to One:** There is approximately one chicken for each human in the world.

BUSY BEES

One bee always seems ready to feed another bee, even if that bee is from a different colony. Bees are very social insects, and mutual feeding seems to be the order of their existence. The workers feed the helpless queen, who cannot feed herself. They feed the drones and, of course, they feed the young. They seem to actually enjoy this social act. They also cluster together for warmth in cold weather and fan their wings to cool the hive in hot weather.

When swarming time comes, bee scouts take flight to find suitable quarters where the new colony can establish itself. These scouts report on its whereabouts by executing a strange dance (as they also do to report the location of honey). After the report, the entire assembly seems to reach a common choice. Then they all take wing in what is called a swarm.

The bee has been aptly described as busy. To produce one tablespoon of honey for our toast, the little bee makes 4,200 trips to flowers. A worker bee will fly as far as eight miles in search of nectar. He makes about 10 trips a day to the fields, each trip lasting 20 minutes and 400 flowers.

To produce just one pound of clover honey, the bee must visit 56,000 clover heads. Since each head has 60 flower tubes, a total of 3,360,000 visits are necessary. In the end, that worker bee will have flown the equivalent of three times around the world.

The bee is more honored than other creatures, not because she labors, but because she labors for others. This is a good model for the church—everybody working to make life sweeter for others! Jesus said the world would recognize the church by our mutual love for each other.

Unfortunately this has not always been the history of God's people.
John 13:35 *"By this shall all men know that ye are my disciples, if ye have love one to another."*

AND DID YOU KNOW...

- **Cow Fact:** It is possible to lead a cow upstairs...but not down-stairs.
- **Duck Noises:** A duck's quack doesn't echo and no one knows why.

BUMBLEBEES

Once called "humblebees" because of their good nature, bumblebees rarely have it in them to sting. But young children struggled to say humblebee, often resorting to "bumblebee." Because of the bumblebee's awkward clumsy movements, the adults adopted the new name.

Bumblebees are among the few insects that can control their body temperature. In cold weather, queens and workers can shiver their flight muscles to warm themselves. Their large size and heat-conserving hairy coats also help them stay warm, allowing them to fly and work in colder climates and lower temperatures than most other insects.

Aviation engineers have studied bumblebees and determined that with their small wings and fat bodies, it is aerodynamically impossible for them to fly. But the bumblebees have not had time to read those reports, so they continue flying.

Philippians 4:13 *"I can do all things through Christ which strengtheneth me."*

WHALES

Among the most incredible creatures on the planet, the blue whale is the heaviest and longest animal on earth. The average adult male is about 82 feet long, with a body weight of up to 120 tons!

A blue whale eats up to four tons of krill every day, which is equivalent to eating a fully grown African elephant. The blue whales also create the highest geyser, blowing water up to 40 feet in the air.

Whales are the deepest divers of any mammal. Early whalers reported some whales with dive times of more than two hours. The sperm whale is the deepest diver, going down 6,500 feet!

The sperm whale also has the world's heaviest brain, which can weigh over 20 pounds (compared to a 3-pound human brain).

Whales do not sleep like humans, but rather rest or catnap on the surface of the sea for a few moments while they are swimming. Each side of the brain takes a turn to 'switch off' while the other half stays vigilant and keeps the animal breathing. When whales open their eyes underwater, special greasy tears protect them from the stinging salt. Whales also live a very long time. One bowhead whale was reported to live 130 years!

The gray whale is believed to undertake the longest migration of any mammal. It swims from its winter breeding grounds in Baja California to its summer feeding grounds in the rich waters of the Bering Sea in the Arctic, and back again. This amounts to a total annual distance of 12,000 miles. In a gray whale's lifetime, this is equivalent to swimming to the moon and back!

Male humpback whales sing the longest and most complex songs in the animal kingdom. Each song lasts for more than half an hour. The aim of the singing is probably to woo females and to warn off rival males. These messages can be heard underwater from more than a thousand miles away!

The Bible tells that God has sent special coded messages of love and warning to man in the book of Revelation.

Revelation 1:3 *"Blessed is he that readeth, and they that hear the words of this prophecy, and keep those things which are written therein: for the time is at hand."*

MAN-EATERS

For nine months between 1898–99, the two infamous "Man-eater lions of Tsavo" terrorized workers employed in the construction of a railway bridge in Uganda. As the death toll rose, construction was brought to a virtual standstill when the workers refused to continue until protection could be provided. Finally, the reign of terror was brought to an end when Lieutenant Colonel J.H. Patterson succeeded in tracking and killing the two lions that had devoured 135 men! The lions are now on permanent display at the

Field Museum in Chicago.

But even more deadly, a tigress in India was reported to have killed and eaten 436 people in 1907 before being killed!

Actually the record for man-eating goes to one lion that has devoured even more than all these others combined!

1 Peter 5:8 "*Be sober, be vigilant; because your adversary the devil, as a roaring lion, walketh about, seeking whom he may devour ...* "

AND DID YOU KNOW...

- **Cricket Fact:** The outdoor temperature can be estimated within a few degrees by timing the chirps of a cricket. Count the number of chirps within a 15 second timeframe and add 37 to the total. The result will be very close to the fahrenheit temp. (Only works in warm weather.)

- **Animal Immunity:** Sharks are the only animal that never gets sick.

POLAR BEARS

Found along the coasts and islands of the northernmost regions, polar bears are the largest land carnivores. In fact, one adult male polar bear weighed more than 2,200 pounds! Yet the young are only about 25 ounces when born. Polar bears, covered with a heavy white fur coat, actually have black skin.

Polar bears also have very large stomachs with a capacity of more than 150 pounds of food, which allows them to go weeks between meals. They are also great roamers, covering up to 50 miles a day and 100,000 square miles during its lifetime in a constant search for seals.

Strong swimmers, polar bears paddle with their large front paws and use their rear paws as rudders to steer. They swim an average of six mph and can go as far as 60 miles without a pause. Polar bears are also excellent divers, remaining submerged for up to two minutes and attain a depth of 15 feet. They have also been observed leaping out of the water up to eight feet in the air to surprise a seal resting on an ice floe.

Pregnant females are the only polar bears that hibernate. When the long dark winter months begin in October, the expecting mother will enter the den to spend up to 170 days in a state of depressed activity known as carnivoran lethargy. While hibernating, a bear's heart rate drops from about 55 beats per minute to only 10 beats per minute. During this time, it's not uncommon for a female polar bear with newborn cubs to lose as much as 40 percent of her weight.

Did you know that the Bible teaches the devil will be forced into a state of dark "carnivoran lethargy" for 1,000 years?

THE SHREW

The smallest animal in the world also has the biggest appetite: it's the mouse-like shrew. One variety in northern Europe called the "least" shrew, which is rarely longer than an inch and a half, can consume the equivalent of its own weight every three hours. In fact, the appetite of the shrew is so voracious and it's metabolism so fast that if they do not eat for two hours, they might starve to death.

Not only is the shrew the smallest animal, it is the most ferocious as well. In its desperate quest to feed its ravenous hunger, the little shrew will attack and eat almost anything that moves— including creatures twice its size!

DRAGONFLIES

Among the fastest of all insects, dragonflies have been clocked at more than 25 mph. Fossils also tell us that before the flood, some dragonflies had wingspans of about 30 inches. And they're strong too! About half of their body mass is devoted to flight muscles, and they have the ability to lift more than twice their bodyweight . . . a feat that no man-made aircraft has ever come near!

Dragonflies can take off backwards, accelerate quickly and then stop in an instant. They can also execute an unbanked turn as if on a pivot, summersault in the heat of combat, and fly virtually any maneuver using an infinite combination of four wings.

Not only can the dragonfly out-maneuver anything else on wings, it can see better too! Its wrap-around compound eyes contain over 30,000 lenses, providing a 360-degree field of view. In fact, a dragonfly can see a gnat three feet away, dart from his nest, seize and devour the prey, and then return to its perch all in about one second. Even the U.S. Air Force has studied the amazing flight versatility of dragonflies in wind tunnels, hoping to uncover the secret of incredible aerodynamic abilities.

Yet the extraordinary flight and sight of dragonflies is nothing in comparison to the spectacular powers of the ministering spirits God has created called angels.

Psalm 91:11 "For he shall give his angels charge over thee, to keep thee in all thy ways."

AND DID YOU KNOW...

- **Scaly Symmetry:** The distance between an alligator's eyes, in inches, is directly proportional to the length of the alligator, in feet.

- **Bear Races:** A full-grown bear can run as fast as a horse.

BUG RECORDS

One species of Australian dragonfly has been clocked at 36 mph. But the fastest moving land insects are the tropical cockroaches, which can move 50 body lengths per second (an equivalent to a human sprinter running the 100 yard dash in 1 second or approximately 200 mph)!

The longest flea jump record belongs to the cat flea, which has been known to leap to a height of 34 inches. While this may not sound impressive, consider that in jumping such an incredible height relative to body size, the flea subjects itself to over 200 g's! Imagine a 100-pound man leaping over 1,000 feet in a second! The g-force he would endure would make him feel as if he weighed 20,000 pounds! In relation, a flea takes off with greater acceleration than the space shuttle!

Psalm 9:1 "I will praise thee, O LORD, with my whole heart; I will shew forth all thy marvellous works."

DOG RECORDS

The world's heaviest and longest dog was an Old English Mastiff named Zorba. In 1989, Zorba weighed 343 pounds and was 8 feet, 3 inches long from nose to tail!

The tallest dog on record was Shamgret Danzas. He was 42 inches tall (at the shoulder!) and weighed 238 pounds. The smallest dog in history was a tiny Yorkie from Blackburn, England. At two years of age and fully grown, this little fur ball weighed only four ounces and was an incredible 2.5 inches tall by 3.75 inches long (approximately the size of a matchbox)!

The oldest dog was an Australian cattle-dog named Bluey. He was put to sleep at the age of 29 years and 5 months.

ELECTRIC EELS

Did you know there is no such thing as an electric "eel?" They are actually fish that emit electrical discharges. The organs adapted for this purpose consist of highly compact nerve-ending groups. In small electric eels, a typical nerve-ending cell is about a quarter-inch long and has an electric voltage of 0.14v. The average small electric eel has about 1,000 of these nerve-ending cells per square inch of skin, which is capable of developing more than 75v per inch. Discharges are emitted in self-defense or to detect or stun their prey while hunting.

The discharge organs of this fish include a small so-called pilot organ, which emits electricity continuously for navigation and a large high-voltage organ that supplies most of the power to the occasional power zaps. The most powerful electric eel discharge is emitted by the eel native to the rivers of the Amazon Basin. They are capable of emitting a discharge of 450 to 600v, which is capable of stunning a horse.

The devil also has the ability to paralyze his victims before he destroys them...

SCORPIONS

The world hosts about 1,400 species of scorpions, with about 40 kinds occurring in the United States. Scorpions, like spiders, have eight legs and belong to the arachnid family. They feed on insects they catch with their two lobster-like claws and kill with a venomous stinger at the end of their segmented, abdominal tail. In most species, the sting is merely painful to humans and not fatal, although the sting of one species found in the States has proved fatal to young children.

But scorpions have been known to kill and devour their own species as well as demonstrate vengeful, even suicidal, behavior. One experimenter placed a hundred of these arachnids in a large glass vessel, and after a few days only 14 remained. The rest had been killed and eaten by the others. He then put a pregnant female in a glass vessel and observed her as she devoured her young as fast as they were born. One managed to escape, taking refuge on the mother's back, and found revenge by killing the mother scorpion in turn. If cornered with no possible escape, a scorpion will sting itself to death. *I'm sad to say I have met some scorpion Christians during my ministry.*

Acts 20:27-30 *"For I have not shunned to declare unto you all the counsel of God. Take heed therefore unto yourselves, and to all the flock, over the which the Holy Ghost hath made you overseers, to feed the church of God, which he hath purchased with his own blood. For I know this, that after my departing shall grievous wolves enter in among you, not sparing the flock. Also of your own selves shall men arise, speaking perverse things, to draw away disciples after them."*

EUROPEAN CUCKOO

Known as a ".brood parasite," the female European Cuckoo lays her eggs in the nests of smaller bird species—like the reed warbler. In turn, these unsuspecting mothers unwittingly incubate, feed and raise the young imposters, typically at the expense of their very own off-spring. One of the tragedies of nature is when a little reed warbler works itself to death to satisfy the voracious hunger of a fat cuckoo chick while her own starving young are crowded out of the nest!

Many don't realize that the devil has laid an egg in the Christian church that has been hatched, adopted and fed until it has grown bigger than life.

Matthew 7:15 *"Beware of false prophets, which come to you in sheep's clothing, but inwardly they are ravening wolves."*

SINGLE-CELL LIFE

The complexity of a single living cell, with all its inner systems, is more intricate and elaborate than all of the complex workings of New York City!

Swiss mathematician Charles Eugene Guye computed the odds of such an occurrence at 10^{160}. (That's 10 multiplied by itself 160 times, a number too large to articulate.) The idea of a living cell coming into existence by chance is as ridiculous as the notion of a mudslide spontaneously producing the Taj Mahal—or a bomb tossed into a junkyard producing a Boeing 777 jumbo jet!

Genesis 1:1, 31 "In the beginning God created the heaven and the earth. ... And God saw every thing that he had made, and, behold, it was very good ... "

AND DID YOU KNOW...

- **Sad Buffalo:** Two hundred years ago, anywhere from 30 to 70 million bison, or buffalo, roamed free in North America. During the late 1800s, commercial hide hunters, settlers, and thrill seekers shot literally millions of bison. This killing spree brought the species to the verge of extinction.

- **Sad Fowl:** Every year in Canada thousands of ducks and other birds die from lead poisoning. They get lead poisoning by eating lead shotgun pellets and lead fishing sinkers and jigs that have fallen into their feeding grounds.

OCTOPUS

Among the most flexible and versatile of all God's creatures, an octopus can squeeze into amazingly small spaces to hunt or avoid predators. They've been known to hide themselves in soft drink cans and aspirin bottles! This ability to fit in tight spots pays off when hunting, as octopuses can chase small crabs, shrimp, and fish into tiny cracks, coaxing them out with their long tentacles.

They also have highly developed brains and demonstrate their amazing intelligence in getting into and out of fishermen's traps. At the same time, octopuses are amazing swimmers, jetting themselves along by squirting a turbo charged burst of water out of a biological jet engine. And when threatened, an octopus can expel a cloudy decoy of dark ink and jet away while changing color, leaving the predator totally confused.

When it comes to disguise, octopus are the ultimate chameleons. Thanks to special cells in their skin, they have the ability to change color and texture, assuming a thousand combinations. In the blink of an eye, they can fade into the sea floor, appearing to be just another bumpy rock. And when it comes time to mate, some octopuses advertise with bright flashes of color sure to attract a partner. Some even put on light shows with glow-in-the-dark tentacles!

One Pacific Ocean octopus has earned its name from its incredible ability to transform its shape. The mimic octopus has been known to imitate everything from giant crabs and fish to sea snakes. One clever species will even take up residence in a vacant clamshell and use the suction cups on its tentacles to slowly open and close the shell. It will then wiggle the tip of one tentacle like a little worm to attract hungry fish—and whoosh—the octopus will jet out and seize the unsuspecting victim.

You can't help but admire the octopus for its versatile and crafty tricks, but he reminds me of another more deadly deceiver!

AND DID YOU KNOW...

- **Football Cows:** It takes 3,000 cows to supply the NFL with enough leather for a year's supply of footballs.

- **Fawn the Cow:** An American cow called Fawn was not afraid of flying. In May 1963, she was swept up by a tornado and carried half a mile, only to land safely in another farmer's field. Five years later, another tornado carried her over a bus. She survived this too, and lived to the ripe old age of 25.

  Romans 8:28 "And we know that all things work together for good to them that love God, to them who are the called according to his purpose."

BLUE WHALES

This giant sea creature eats tons of food a day but has no teeth, lives in the ocean all its life but breathes air, and is the largest of earth's animals but is endangered. It's smaller than the head of a pin when it's conceived, but eleven months later will weigh more than two tons and is 24 feet long!

For the first eight months, the mother provides its only food. Her milk is so rich that the baby blue whale can gain up to nine pounds in one hour. After that, the blue whale will grow to about 50 feet long—longer than a greyhound bus. Blue whales eat mostly a shrimp-like creature called krill. An adult whale will eat one to two tons a day.

A blue whale is not considered full-grown until 10 years of age, when its heart will be as big as a small car and its blood vessels large enough for a human baby to crawl through. The average length will be 75 to 90 feet long and weigh up to 170 tons. The heaviest blue whale ever weighed was 209 tons, as heavy as 27 elephants. The longest blue whale measured was just over 110 feet long, as long as a row of 7 minivans.

No one is sure exactly how long whales live, but one was found with a 130-year-old spearhead in its blubber. Scientists believe that the number of blue whales alive now has dropped from the 200,000 before whale hunting to less than 10,000.

The blue whale makes a unique four-note call to signal the other whales in case of danger. This call is the loudest sound made by any living creature (over 150 decibels) and can be heard hundreds of miles across entire oceans.

God has made provision for humans to communicate with Him at great distance. It's called prayer, and Jesus gave us two very important examples.

Mark 11:25, 26 "And when ye stand praying, forgive, if ye have ought against any: that your Father also which is in heaven may forgive you your trespasses. But if ye do not forgive, neither will your Father which is in heaven forgive your trespasses."

GREYFRIARS BOBBY

Near Greyfriars Churchyard in Edinburgh, Scotland, stands a memorial fountain and statue to a little skye-terrier dog named Greyfriars Bobby. In the 1850s, a kindly shepherd named Jock Gray made his way in from the meadows with Bobby to the local inn each day at one o'clock. At the café, Jock would eat lunch as Bobby laid at his feet chewing a bone tucked under his paw.

The daily tradition went on for many years, but ended when old

Jock collapsed and died. When he was buried in the Greyfriars Churchyard cemetery, his faithful little dog mournfully watched and marked the spot where his old master was committed to the grave. A few days after the funeral, the proprietor of the inn was surprised when the little terrier showed up at one o' clock begging for a bone. The kind man gave him a roll and a bone, but the same thing happened the following day, and the next, and the next.

On the fourth day, when Bobby finished his afternoon bun and bone, the owner followed the little shepherd dog through town—to the Greyfriars Churchyard. There, Bobby lay down at his master's tombstone. And so for the next 14 years, day and night, rain or shine, until his own death in 1872, the loyal little canine virtually lived on top of his master's grave. The little terrier left the site for only an hour at a time to visit his two friends, the restaurateur who fed him and the sexton who built a shelter for him at the cemetery.

During that 14-year vigil, thousands visited the yard to see this faithful little dog keeping his watch where he last saw his master. In tribute to his lifelong loyalty and devotion, they buried him in the church graveyard beside his master and erected a memorial in his honor.

We are inspired by the loyalty of this little pooch that could not forget the burial place of his master, but did you know the Bible teaches that there is a grave that God forgets about right after the funeral?

Psalm 34: 15-17 "The eyes of the LORD *are upon the righteous, and his ears are open unto their cry. The face of the* LORD *is against them that do evil, to cut off the remembrance of them from the earth. The righteous cry, and the* LORD *heareth, and delivereth them out of all their troubles."*

ANTS

The most numerous creatures on earth, the combined weight of every ant is greater than the combined weight of all humans, making up one-tenth of the world's total animal tissue.

Strong in relation to their size, ants can carry 10 to 20 times their body weight and work in teams to move extremely heavy things. And if a man could run, pound for pound, as fast as an ant, he could run as fast as a racehorse. Extremely tenacious, ants can even survive up to two days underwater, and they also never sleep!

These little creatures have the largest brain amongst insects in proportion to their size. Their mushroom-shaped brains contain about 250,000 brain cells and function similar to human brains. (A human brain has 10,000 million cells, so in theory, a colony of 40,000 ants has collectively the same size brain as a human. How does it feel to know you are as smart as a hill of ants?) Extremely social, ants also share these activities with humans:

- Livestock Farming: Ants herd aphids like sheep and "milk" them for nectar-like food.
- Cultivation: They grow and store underground gardens for food.
- Child Care: They tenderly feed young and provide intensive nursery care, all while maintaining a careful climate control of 77-degrees Fahrenheit for developing ants.
- Education: Younger ants are taught tricks of the trade.
- Civic Duties: They respond and organize for massive group projects.
- Military Forces: Ants raise an army of specialized soldiers to ward off other insects, animals and other threats. In fact, one type of ant called the "slave-maker" raids the nests of other ants and steals their eggs. When these new ants hatch, they are forced to work within the colony.
- Earth Movers: Ants are great earthmovers, moving little mountains every day.
- Engineers: They can also tunnel from two directions and meet exactly midway.
- Flood Control: They incorporate water traps to keep out rain.
- Communications: Ants have a complex tactile and chemical communication system.
- Career Specialization: Ants change and learn new careers. Some clean, some forage, some care for the young, and some are guards or scouts.

But as intelligent and resourceful as they are, ants cannot survive alone. They can only exist and thrive as part of a colony. *Likewise, the Bible teaches that Christians will only thrive as part of a church family.*

I Corinthians 12:12, 14-27 "For as the body is one, and hath many members, and all the members of that one body, being many, are one body: so also is Christ … For the body is not one member, but many. If the foot shall say, Because I am not the hand, I am not of the body; is it therefore not of the body? And if the ear shall say, Because I am not the eye, I am not of the body; is it therefore not of the body? If the whole body were an eye, where were the hearing? If the whole were hearing, where were the smelling? But now hath God set the members every one of them in the body, as it hath pleased him. And if they were all one member, where were the body? But now are they many members, yet but one body. And the eye cannot say unto the hand, I have no need of thee: nor again the head to the feet, I have no need of you. Nay, much more those members of the body, which seem to be more feeble, are necessary: And those members of the body, which we think to be less honourable, upon these we bestow more abundant honour; and our uncomely parts have more abundant comeliness. For our comely parts have no need: but God hath tempered the body together, having given more abundant honour to that part which lacked; That there should be no schism in the body; but that the members should have the same care one for another. And whether one member suffer, all the members suffer with it; or one member be honoured, all the members rejoice with it. Now ye are the body of Christ, and members in particular."

THE BARN OWL

This most interesting of God's creatures can be found on every continent (except Antarctica of course!). This is partly due to the abundance of the barn owl's favorite food: mice. Owls have no teeth, so they swallow their mice whole. The indigestible parts, like fur, bones and teeth are compressed into a pellet that is ejected by mouth.

Owls are excellent hunters, because they have very large eyes that are especially keen under low light. The wise-appearing, forward-facing eyes, which account for five percent of their body weight, offer a wide range of binocular vision. In fact, they're not even eyeballs, but rather elongated tubes like short telescopes held in place by bony structures in the skull. For this reason, an owl cannot "roll" or move its eyes, but only look straight ahead! However, it more than compensates for this with the ability to turn its head around and almost upside-down. It achieves this with a long and flexible neck with 14 vertebrae, twice as many as humans. This allows the owl to turn its head a range of 270 degrees, just short of the full circle as many believe it capable of.

When a typical bird flies, air rushes over the surface of the wing, creating turbulence, which makes a whooshing or flapping noise. But barn owls are absolutely silent when they fly. A velvety layer on the feather surface muffles sound. In addition, the leading edges of the wing feathers have a fine comb that deadens the sound of the wing beats. The silent flight prevents prey from hearing its approach and aids the owl's hearing, which is extremely acute.

Strangely, its ear openings are at slightly different levels on its head and are set at different angles—one high up near the owl's forehead and the other lower, about level with the bird's nostrils. The lopsided placement helps these hunters precisely pinpoint prey. The ears are also surrounded by feathers that can be opened up to catch the faint sounds of small prey or closed down to protect against loud sounds. They are covered by a flexible ruff made up of short, densely webbed feathers that frames the face, turning it into a parabolic dish-like reflector for sound. This gives the owl very sensitive and directional hearing with which it can locate even small prey, even in total darkness.

The Bible teaches us that the eyes of God can see us wherever we are—and His ears can even hear our thoughts.

WATER BEARS

A tiny animal, less than a millimeter long, can withstanding the most extreme conditions on earth. This arthropod, commonly called a water bear, is probably living in your garden right now.

Its proper name is a *tar-de-grade*, and there are many species found all over the world, from the coldest poles to the warmest jungle. The beast has eight legs, two eyes, a central nervous system, and has piercing mouthparts that it uses to feed on the juices of plants. It is just barely visible to the naked eye.

So how tough are these guys? They normally live in damp places like mosses and lichens, but these habitats often dry out, get baked in the sun, and freeze in winter. So to survive these un-cozy periods, the water bear has a clever trick. It pulls in its legs, loses some water, shrivels up, and transforms into a "tun," enabling it to withstand all kinds of extremes while hibernating.

Here's a sample of some harsh environments that a water bear has survived:

- Left in a bottle with dried moss for 120 years without water or air—when water was added, they sprang to life.
- Exposed to -458 degrees fahrenheit, the coldest temperature possible (i.e., one degree above "absolute zero"). When thawed, they started up again.
- Exposed to pressure six times greater than the deepest ocean. When brought to the surface, they began tooling around.
- Exposed to radiation 1,000 times more than enough to kill a human. They survived.

In fact, water bears are theoretically capable of surviving a space journey without artificial protection. It's also one of the few animals that can have its photograph taken in an electron microscope and live to tell the tale.

The Bible teaches that there is only one other creature more durable than the water bear. "When you pass through the waters, I will be with you; And through the rivers, they shall not overflow you. When you walk through the fire, you shall not be burned, Nor shall the flame scorch you." (Isaiah 43:2).

MORE AMAZING ANIMAL FACTS - DID YOU KNOW...

- When opossums play 'possum, they aren't playing—they actually pass out from sheer terror?

- All owls lay white eggs?

- The duck most often depicted on the "Duck Stamp" is the mallard—six times?

- The world's termites outweigh the world's humans 10 to 1?

- A cockroach can live for nine days without its head?

- White cockatoos are the only parrots that can be sexed by eye color; females have a visible pupil, while males have black irises?

- While drug-sniffing dogs are trained to bark like crazy and go "aggressive" at the first whiff of the right powder, bomb-sniffing dogs are trained to go "passive" lest they set off a motion sensor, noise sensor, or any number of other things that might trigger a bomb?

- The snapping turtle eats carrion and is used by police to find dead bodies in lakes, ponds, and swamps?

- The "Ragdoll" is the largest breed of domesticated cat in the world, with adult males averaging 22 to 25 pounds?

- The smallest fish is the *Trimattum Nanus* of the Chagos Archipelago. It measures 0.33 inches?

- Ferrets sleep for 20 hours a day?

- A bear only hibernates in a cave with an opening to the north slope, unless it dwells in the southern hemisphere?

- In New Zealand, a two-foot long bird called a Kea eats the strips of rubber around car windows?
- A group of geese on the ground is a gaggle, a group of geese in the air is a skein?
- A crocodile always grows new teeth to replace the old teeth?
- Porcupines float in water?
- The sloth (a mammal) moves so slowly that green algae can grow undisturbed on its fur?
- A hedgehog's heart beats 300 times a minute?
- Camels have three eyelids to protect themselves from blowing sand?
- There are 2,500 different species of ants in the world?
- The placement of a donkey's eyes in its head enables it to see all four feet at all times?
- A mole can dig a tunnel 300 feet long in just one night?
- A hippo can open its mouth wide enough to fit a 4-foot tall child inside?
- A hummingbird weighs less than a penny?
- Over 10,000 birds a year die from smashing into windows?
- There are more than one million animal species on earth?

Contents:
Psalm 118 • Armageddon

PSALM 118

Here are some interesting facts about one of David's songs for the Lord:

• It's the middle chapter of the entire Bible.
• Psalm 117 is the shortest chapter in the Bible, and Psalm 119 is the longest.
• The Bible has 594 chapters before Psalm 118 & 594 chapters after it.
• Add up all the chapters except Psalm 118, and you get a total of 1,188 chapters.
• Psalm 118 verse 8 is the middle verse of the entire Bible.

And should the central verse not have a fairly important message? *"It is better to take refuge in the* LORD *than to trust in man"* (**Psalm 118:8**), which is perhaps the central theme of the entire Bible.

ARMAGEDDON

This scary word is an enigma for most Bible scholars. It only appears once in Scripture *(Revelation 16:16)* and is found nowhere else in Greek writings. Many believe it is connected with the valley or hill of Megiddo, but that verse in *Revelation* says the word comes from *"the Hebrew tongue."* Bible translator and scholar Robert Moffat argues strongly that the word is really referring to the battle of Gideon, when a small but divinely chosen guard gained the victory over a powerful and vastly larger enemy.

Armageddon comes from the Hebrew *"amar gid'own,"* which can be translated from *"yehovah 'amar gid'own"* (**Judges 7:2**) or "The Word or Challenge of Jehovah to Gideon" (*Strong's Concordance*). It's also noteworthy that the battle of Gideon was fought in the valley of Megiddo.

INCREDIBLE BIOLOGY

Contents:

Ancient Seeds • Seeds • Frankincense • Trees • The Bristlecone Pine • Tobacco • Four-Leaf Clover • The Thistle Emblem

ANCIENT SEEDS

The oldest known viable seeds were found in 1954 in a lemming burrow in Canada's frigid Yukon. The frozen burrow, buried in silt and sediment, was 4,200 years old. The arctic tundra lupine seeds were found with lemming remains, and when placed in favorable conditions, several seeds sprouted within 48 hours. One of the plants later bloomed.

Water lily seeds have also been found with a canoe that had been buried in a bog near Tokyo for more than 3,000 years. Scientists have also discovered that seeds from the oriental lotus plant have germinated some 3,000 years after their dispersal.

Another case of extremely old seeds that sprouted was 3,400-year-old beans from the tomb of Tutankhamen. English Egyptologist Howard Carter found the seeds when he excavated the famous tomb in 1922. Among the many rich objects in the tomb, he found the bean seeds after they'd been asleep underground for 3,300 years. He had them planted in the ground in rich soil, with sun, fertilizer and water—they sprouted and grew into healthy plants.

It is astonishing how the Lord can design seeds to quietly store the essence of life for thousands of years and then spring into existence with a little light and water. The Bible teaches that people can find new life under the right conditions even after being "spiritually" buried!

SEEDS

A turnip seed, under good conditions, can increase its weight 15 times a minute—and in rich soil, after sprouting, they can increase their weight up to 15,000 times a day!

The world's largest seeds resemble giant coconuts, and for centuries were thought to come from the sea because they often washed up on the shores around the Indian Ocean. Consequently, those who found them called them sea coconuts. But in the 18th century, the seeds were discovered to come from tall nut palms that grew only on the Seychelles Islands. For years, Eastern kings and Oriental potentates eagerly sought the seeds, which weigh upwards of 40 pounds, thinking they could be used as antidotes to poison.

Still, there is no seed force more powerful than a growing squash seed. An 18-day-old squash was harnessed on a lever and lifted 50 pounds as it grew! Nineteen days later, it raised 5,000 pounds!

*Perhaps this is why Jesus said, "If you have faith as a mustard seed, you can move mountains" (**Matthew 17:20**). But what is this seed of faith that can move mountains?*

AND DID YOU KNOW...

• **Always:** Honey is the only food that doesn't spoil.

• **Potato Fact:** In the United States, a pound of potato chips costs 200 times more then a pound of potatoes.

FRANKINCENSE

One of the three gifts offered to baby Jesus, frankincense is a fragrant resin that is found in some of the world's harshest places—Oman, Yemen, and Somalia. The spindly trees themselves are actually disappointing to behold. They are lowly, twisted, thorny things with fat prickly branches spreading out into small crinkly leaves.

Yet as soon as an incision is made into the silvery bark, brilliant drops of white resin ooze from the wound. These drops, known as luban, are left on the tree for two weeks to dry. Then the little pearls are gathered in the early morning. From Rome to India, frankincense was deemed one of the most prized substances in the civilized world, worth its weight in gold. It was essential for a host of uses, ranging from religious to cosmetic to medicinal. Besides a lovely fragrance, frankincense is attributed with healing powers, which range from treatment of depression and irritability to physical ailments such as eczema.

Frankincense was also used to embalm corpses. When the tomb of Tutankhamen was opened in 1922, one of the sealed flasks still released the scent even after 3,300 years! In fact, ancient records report that embalmers of old did not fall prey to the diseases from which their clients died. Much later, during the time of the Black Death in England, it was also noted that perfumers seemed to be immune to plague. This could be why Arabic doctors made sure that their clothes were strongly scented with frankincense when they visited patients. According to ancient documents, frankincense was used in staggering quantities—the annual consumption of incense in the temple of Baal at Babylon was 2.5 tons!

The frankincense trade peaked in the Roman Empire in the first century. Nero burned it by the ton at religious ceremonies. To supply the copious need, this rare resin had to be carried overland via long and incredibly grueling journeys. Eventually, the incense caravans grew in size to 3,000 camels in one procession! Even today, satellite images still reveal faint traces of these ancient caravan trails carved in the wilderness. The trade was so lucrative that Alexander the Great planned to invade Arabia in an effort to control and tax the roads, a plan thwarted only by his death.

While frankincense is a wonderful fragrance, and appears to have some medical value, it's great worth was attached more to its religious purposes. You see, the majority of the great civilizations in the ancient world believed that their prayers could only be carried to heaven in the smoke of this sacred incense. No wonder they would pay a king's ransom for the powder. The Bible also teaches that there is one true vehicle that will transport our prayers to heaven.

Romans 8:26 *"Likewise the Spirit also helpeth our infirmities: for we know not what we should pray for as we ought: but the Spirit itself maketh intercession for us with groanings which cannot be uttered."*

TREES

The world's tallest tree is still a matter for conjecture. In 1872, in Victoria, Australia, lumberjacks felled a mountain ash that was believed to have been 500 ft. tall. But there is no official record of this.

There are other claims that the tallest-ever title should go to a Douglas fir cut down in British Columbia in 1940—said to have measured 417 feet. But the tallest non-sequoia alive today is also a Douglas fir at Quinault Lake Park Trail, Washington, at 310 feet.

The stoutest living tree is in the Mexican state of Oaxaca. A Montezuma cypress called the Santa Maria del Tule has a girth of 113 feet—with a height of 141 feet. Its age is guessed at anywhere from 4,000 to 6,000 years. And in 1770, a European chestnut, known as the Chestnut of the Hundred Horses, measuring 204 feet in circumference, was found on the edge of Mount Etna in Sicily.

The seeds of all these tremendous trees weigh only about $1/6000^{th}$ of an ounce.

The oldest tree recorded was a 4,900-year-old bristlecone pine in Wheeler Peak, eastern California. It was cut down with a chain saw in 1964. The oldest living tree today is also a bristlecone called Methuselah, estimated at 4,600 years in California's White Mountains.

And the most massive living thing on earth is a tree, weighing an estimated 2,145 tons with a true girth of 79 feet. It stands in Sequoia National Park, California, and is called General Sherman. The famous Zaman tree in Venezuela, though not unusual in height or girth, had an enormous branch spread that yielded a shade with a circumference of 614 feet (and every bough was festooned with orchids). A sycamore in Indiana with a height of 150 feet and a girth of over 42 feet has been called the largest shade tree in America.

The combined length of the roots of a large oak would total several hundred miles. The giant saguaro of the southwest desert region spreads its roots laterally as much as 50 feet underground from the trunk. Hair-like as some tree roots are, an entire system of them exerts a tremendous pressure.

Psalm 1:1-3 "Blessed is the man that walketh not in the counsel of the ungodly, nor standeth in the way of sinners, nor sitteth in the seat of the scornful. But his delight is in the law of the LORD; and in his law doth he meditate day and night. And he shall be like a tree planted by the rivers of water, that bringeth forth his fruit in his season; his leaf also shall not wither; and whatsoever he doeth shall prosper."

Psalm 92:12 "The righteous shall flourish like the palm tree: he shall grow like a cedar in Lebanon."

AND DID YOU KNOW...

• The Sitka Spruce is Britain's most commonly planted tree.

BRISTLECONE PINE

This Great Basin tree can live more than 4,000 years, and one estimated at 4,600 is believed to be among the oldest living trees on the planet. This tree was around when the Egyptians were building the pyramids!

Some of these ancient evergreens found on lonely mountain tops have weathered thousands of years of intense freezing wind, pounding rain, scorching sun, and violent electrical storms. How have they managed to survive through millennia of harsh adverse weather? They send their roots deep, wrap them tenaciously around a solid rock and hang on.

Jesus has clearly foretold that there will be a time of trouble coming upon the world just before His return ... unlike anything in history. This tribulation will be so intense and frightening that if it were not cut short, no life on earth would survive.

THE FOUR-LEAF CLOVER

Working its way into history around 200 B.C. in the British Isles, the sun worshiping Druid priests considered the four-leaf clover a sacred artifact.

Since the clover is typically a three-leaf plant, finding the rare four-leaf variety made it special and mystical. Druids believed that anyone in possession of a four-leaf clover could sense demons and cast spells to offer protec-

tion from their evil presence. It is from this belief that the four-leaf clover became known as a good luck charm. These stories are tracked back through Irish folklore all the way to the writings of Julius Caesar; however, with the advances of modern day science, four-leaf clovers are no longer such a rare find.

In the 1950s, horticulturists developed a seed that sprouts only four-leaf clovers, and today four-leaf clovers are grown by the millions in greenhouses around the world. But while the four-leaf clover has lost much of its natural uniqueness, its charm in Irish legend remains unchanged.

But now a dilemma—Saint Patrick was reported to use the three-leaf clover (or shamrock) as an illustration of the Trinity, which led to its place as the Irish national symbol. But now the Catholic Church is seriously considering exalting Mary, the mother of Jesus, to the status of co-redeemer with the rest of the Godhead. If the Church adds Mary to the Trinity, they will have a holy Quartet ... and then Ireland may have to change its flag to the four-leaf clover. But does the Bible teach that Mary should be revered or deified as a Co-Savior with Jesus?

TOBACCO

This leafy product was once considered a cure for many ailments, including headache, toothache, arthritis, stomach aches, wounds and bad breath. It was made into a tea and even rolled into pills to serve as a medicinal herb. A Spanish doctor, Nicolas Monardes, first described its medicinal potential in a 1577 book called *Joyful News out of the New Found World*, and his views were accepted for more than 200 years.

THE THISTLE EMBLEM

A great Danish army invaded Scotland many years ago. They crept on stealthily over the border and prepared to make a night attack on Scottish forces. There lay the camp of the Scots, silent in the starlight, never dreaming that danger was so near. The Danes, to make their advance quieter, came forward barefooted.

But as they neared the sleeping Scots, one unlucky Dane brought his broad foot down squarely on a bristling thistle. Consequently, a roar of pain followed, and it rang like a trumpet blast through the sleeping camp. In a moment, the Scott soldiers all grabbed their weapons and the Danes were thoroughly routed. From that time, the thistle became the national emblem of Scotland.

Proverbs 16:19 "Better it is to be of an humble spirit with the lowly, than to divide the spoil with the proud."

Luke 14:11 "For whosoever exalteth himself shall be abased; and he that humbleth himself shall be exalted."

James 4:10 "Humble yourselves in the sight of the Lord, and he shall lift you up."

God has His uses for even the simplest and humblest of us.

THE PHENOMENAL HUMAN BODY

Contents:

THE TONGUE

Like the heart, the tongue is almost all muscle. But unlike the repetitive cardiac contractions, it's capable of very precise, complicated and elaborate movements.

The tongue has intrinsic muscle fibers, which run vertically, transversely and longitudinally, allowing a great range of movement. It has many important responsibilities that we usually take for granted. For instance, the tongue is necessary for all speech; no matter what language, the organ is crucial in creating sounds that make up the letters and words spoken. Without a tongue there would be no talking, no singing, no whistling.

Second, we need it to eat. The upper surface is covered with small projections called papilla, which give it a rough texture. This design helps the tongue move food around in the mouth and direct it to your throat. Without your tongue, you would have to lay back to eat.

Third, the tongue is the source of one of your most favorite senses: the sense of taste! It is covered with approximately 10,000 taste buds, grouped in different areas sensitive to sweet, sour, salty and bitter flavors. The sense of smell adds information, providing a wide range of taste. Imagine food with no taste; that's what it would be without your tongue. Chemicals from the food we eat stimulate receptors in each of these areas, and nerves transmit this input to the brain.

Life would be pretty dull without a tongue. The tongue does get a lot of recognition: we often hear phrases like tongue-in-cheek, tongue tied, and tongue twister. And the Bible says the tongue became a subject of confusion and controversy in one of the New Testament churches.

Psalm 34:13 "*Keep thy tongue from evil, and thy lips from speaking guile.*"

Psalm 39:1 "*I said, I will take heed to my ways, that I sin not with my tongue: I will keep my mouth with a bridle, while the wicked is before me.*"

AND DID YOU KNOW...

• **Rare People:** Only one person in 2 billion will live to be 116 or older.

• **Pen Chewers Beware:** On average, 100 people choke to death on ball-point pens every year.

• **Toe Frostbite:** State with the highest percentage of people who walk to work: Alaska

• **Metal Shampoo:** Intelligent people have more zinc and copper in their hair.

• **Orange Irony:** The voice of Bugs Bunny was allergic to carrots.

THE HEART

A tenaciously hard-working dynamo, the heart can continue beating even when all surrounding nerves are severed. And what a beat! It thumps an average of 75 times a minute, 40 million times a year, and 2.5 billion times in an average life.

With each beat, the adult heart discharges about four ounces of blood. This amounts to 3,000 gallons a day or 650,000 gallons a year—enough to fill more than 818,000-gallon tanks. In fact, the heart produces enough energy in one hour to lift a 150-pound man to the top of a three-story building, in 12 hours to lift 65 tons one foot off the ground, and enough power in 70 years to lift the largest battleship completely out of the water. *But despite all the power of a human heart, it is powerless to change itself.*

Ezekiel 11:19 "*Then I will give them one heart, and I will put a new spirit within them, and take the stony heart out of their flesh, and give them a heart of flesh, ...*" *(NKJV)*

PROLIFIC MOTHERS

The most children ever born to one mother took place in the 18th century in Shuya, Russia, near Moscow. In a total of 27 pregnancies, the wife of a peasant named Feodor Vassilyev gave birth to 69 children. The litters were comprised of 16 pairs of twins, seven sets of triplets, and four sets of quadruplets! The case was reported to Moscow by the Monastery of Nikolskiy on February 27, 1782. Only two of the children born died in infancy. Among all their children, there were no single births.

Currently, the world's most prolific mother is Leontina Albina nee Espinosa, of San Antonio, Chile, who in 1981 produced her 55th and last child. Her husband, Gerardo Seconda Albina, states that they were married in Argentina in 1943 and had five sets of triplets (all boys) before coming to Chile.

AND DID YOU KNOW...

- **DNA:** Calculating DNA length for each person, it would stretch across the diameter of the solar system. If the information contained in the DNA could be written down, it would fill a 1,000-volume encyclopedia.

- **Smelly Battle Zone:** The Stasi collected the "smells" of their enemies so that their dogs could find them.

- **South Paw Blues:** More than 2,500 left-handed people a year are killed from using products made for right-handed people.

- **Fattening Mail:** Licking a stamp is consuming 1/10th of a calorie.

- **Dream Land:** The average person has over 1,460 dreams a year.

TYPING IMPAIRED

Tests show that after drinking three bottles of beer, there is an average of 13 percent net memory loss. After taking only small quantities of alcohol, trained typists were tested and their errors increased 40 percent. Only one ounce of alcohol increases the time required to make a decision by nearly 10 percent; hinders muscular reaction by 17 percent; increases errors due to lack of attention by 35 percent.

—*Paul Harvey*

Proverbs 23:19-21 "*Hear, my son, and be wise; and guide your heart in the way. Do not mix with winebibbers, or with gluttonous eaters of meat; for the drunkard and the glutton will come to poverty, and drowsiness will clothe a man with rags.*" *(NKJV)*

Proverbs 20:1 "*Wine is a mocker, intoxicating drink arouses brawling, and whoever is led astray by it is not wise.*" *(NKJV)*

AND DID YOU KNOW...

- **Pass the Cornflakes:** The average North American will eat about 11.9 pounds of cereal per year.

- **Bed Potatoes:** You burn more calories sleeping than you do watching television.

- **Fruit Benefits:** Apples are more efficient than coffee at waking you up in the morning.

- **Gross Fact:** Most dust particles in your house are made from dead skin.

- **Blind Nations:** All U.S. Presidents have worn glasses. Some just didn't like being seen wearing them in public.

- **Celery Diet:** Celery has negative calories. It takes more energy to eat celery then celery has to begin with.

EYES

To simulate one-hundredth of a second of the complete processing of even a single nerve cell from the human eye requires several minutes of processing time on a supercomputer. The human eye has 10 million or more such cells constantly interacting with each other in  complex ways. This means it would take a minimum of 100 years of supercomputer processing to simulate what takes place in your eye many times every second. Source: *Missouri Association for Creation*

Psalm 92:5 "*O LORD, how great are thy works! And thy thoughts are very deep.*"

AND DID YOU KNOW...

- That you're born with 300 bones, but only have 206 when you die?
- That human thigh bones are stronger than concrete?
- The liquid inside young coconuts can substitute for blood plasma?
- Nerve impulses to and from the brain travel as fast as 170 miles per hour.

HUMAN TOUCH

In 1915, Dr. Henry D. Chapin found that in infant-care homes throughout the United States, nearly every child under two years died. Knowing that babies were adequately nourished and cleaned, he wondered how an almost 100 percent mortality rate could be explained? He then discovered the policy of "no coddling." Babies were dying from a lack of touch.

During World War II, an orphanage in London (a warehouse for a wave of unwanted babies) gave children only obvious essential care such as clothing, food, and shelter. It was all they could do just to attend to the babies' physical needs. The infant mortality rate was just 50 percent. They simply did not know then the importance that touch plays in the physical and emotional well-being of babies.

Someone eventually came up with the idea of touching the babies more. Thus, the order was given to any and all workers, from the janitor to the director, to reach down and stroke or gently touch every baby they passed in the course of their day. They were not required to pick them up or spend any significant amount of time—they simply had to touch. The results of this new mandate were astonishing: Within a two-year period, the mortality rate dropped to 15 percent.

The 13th century historian Salimbene describes a terrible experiment ordered by German Emperor Frederick II. The emperor wanted to know what language a child would speak if raised without hearing any words. So babies were taken from their mothers and raised in isolation. The result: They all died. Salimbene wrote in 1248, "They could not live without caressing." Nor can anyone else. Human babies definitely need tender-loving care to survive.

Untouched adults might not die, but they will experience emotional and social atrophy. Could this be why everywhere Jesus went, He touched people? Whether He was blessing children or healing a leper, Jesus made it a point to reach out and lovingly touch people.

Mark 10:13 *"Then they brought young children to Him, that He should touch them: ... "*

Matthew 8:3 *"And Jesus put forth his hand, and touched him, saying, I will; be thou clean. And immediately his leprosy was cleansed."*

Matthew 8:15 *"And he touched her hand, and the fever left her ... "*

Matthew 20:34 *"So Jesus had compassion on them, and touched their eyes: and immediately their eyes received sight, and they followed him."*

Contents:

SR-71 BLACKBIRD

Long before such a feat of engineering would have been thought possible, Lockheed Aircraft designed and built the most impressive aircraft to ever roam the skies. The first flight of an SR-71 "Blackbird" took place in 1964, and they officially entered service in January 1966.

For years, the Blackbird's maximum speed and altitude was kept top secret. But we now know the aircraft set two world records for absolute speed (2,193 miles per hour) and altitude (more than 85,068 feet). At those dizzying heights and speeds, you can understand why the pair of pilots had to wear pressurized space suits.

For more than 30 years, the SR-71 flew with impunity. A normal cruising speed of Mach 3 and altitude of 80,000 feet, no missile or plane, then or now, could catch it. As a result, despite hundreds of reconnaissance missions over hostile enemy territory, not a single aircraft was lost to enemy fire.

The Blackbird could fly from Los Angeles to Washington D.C. in one hour! And it flew so fast that to refuel in-flight, the sleek jet had to fly as slow as possible and the refueling aircraft as fast as it could to prevent from being run over! The capabilities of the steel bird have not been surpassed: It could survey 100,000 square miles per hour.

The SR-71 was retired in 1990, although it saw temporary reinstatement after Gulf War reconnaissance shortcomings. Even with all the amazing advances in modern aviation technology since, no aircraft can fly faster or higher than the Blackbird. Sadly, President Clinton relegated the world's fastest and highest jet that ever flew to the care of a number of museums around the country in 1999.

It seems like such a tragic waste of potential, power and designing genius to have these wonders of the sky chained to the ground and rusting in museums. *Sadder still is when millions of people go through their lives chained to sin when God designed them to fly.*

Romans 8:21 "Because the creature itself also shall be delivered from the bondage of corruption into the glorious liberty of the children of God."

AND DID YOU KNOW...

- **Sleep Tight:** In Shakespeare's time, mattresses were secured on bed frames by ropes. When you pulled on the ropes the mattress tightened, making the bed firmer to sleep on, thus "good night, sleep tight."

- **Morse Code Nightmare:** The sentence "The quick fox jumps over the lazy brown dog" uses every letter in the alphabet. It was developed by Western Union to test telex/twx communications.

FACIAL RECOGNITION

Forget ID badges, passwords and access cards. To get in and out of your office, you might soon be using something you can't forget or misplace: your face!

Facial recognition technology (FRT), once the subject of science fiction, has appeared in real-life at government buildings and public places. Cameras capture images of people who walk by, and then software matches those pictures with images stored in a database.

Institutions needing greater security, like banks and government offices, have recently incorporated facial recognition to verify identity. Currently, more than 100 casinos across the country have FRT in operation, and the city of Tampa, Florida, uses it in outdoor cameras to spot missing children and lawbreakers.

University scientists have been working on facial recognition for a decade, with financial support from the U.S. Defense Department, in an attempt to develop technology to spot criminals or terrorists at airports and border crossings. Companies began commercializing the technology in the mid 90s. It even made headlines when authorities admitted using it at the Super Bowl to search for felons and terrorists among the crowd of 100,000 spectators.

Electronic readers can be affixed to entryways, keyboards, laptops, and even mobile phones. Here's how it works: FRT software measures a face according to its peaks and valleys—the tip of the nose, the depth of the eye sockets—which are known as nodal points. A human face has 80 nodal points, but the program needs only 14 to 22 to achieve recognition with 99 percent accuracy. The program concentrates on the inner region of the face, which runs from temple to temple and just over the lip (called the "golden triangle").

The use of FRT has upset many politicians and citizens, who call covertly scanning people's faces an invasion of privacy—some high-ranking officials blasted the program's Orwellian aspects. But developers argue that the technology is useless if your picture isn't in the database, and the database isn't storing new faces. They claim no one's privacy is at stake; still it's spooky to think of the growing number of cameras scanning faces and watching our every move. *But did you know the Bible teaches that this technology has actually been around for thousands of years?*

Luke 12: 6-8 "Are not five sparrows sold for two farthings, and not one of them is forgotten before God? But even the very hairs of your head are all numbered. Fear not therefore: ye are of more value than many sparrows. Also I say unto you, Whosoever shall confess me before men, him shall the Son of man also confess before the angels of God."

AND DID YOU KNOW...

- **Unrepeatable:** The only 15-letter word that can be spelled without repeating a letter is uncopyrightable.

- **Book Worm:** The Main Library at Indiana University sinks over an inch every year because when it was built, engineers failed to take into account the weight of all the books that would occupy the building.

- **Rule of Thumb:** This phrase is derived from an old English law that stated that you couldn't beat your wife with anything wider than your thumb.

SPACE SHUTTLE

With a combined thrust of about 5.8 million pounds, solid rocket boosters (SRBs) provide most of the power for the first two minutes of shuttle flight. The SRBs take the space shuttle to an altitude of 28 miles at a staggering speed of 3094 mph before they separate and fall back into the ocean to be retrieved and prepared for another flight.

After the boosters fall away, the three main engines clustered at the rear end of the orbiter continue to provide thrust. They fire for only eight minutes for each flight—just until the shuttle reaches orbit. They have a shelf-life of about 55 flights. Shuttle engines weigh less than 7,000 pounds a piece, but each one puts out almost a half-million pounds of thrust. Pound for pound, they are the world's most powerful rocket engines. In fact, each engine is as powerful as seven Hoover Dams!

For its fiery reentry, the underbelly of the orbiter is protected by 24,000 heat-resistant tiles that must be installed individually by hand. These silicate fiber tiles are incredibly lightweight, about the density of balsa wood, and can last 100 missions before requiring replacement. Each tile can dissipate heat so quickly that a white-hot tile with a temperature of 2300 degrees can be taken from an oven and held in bare hands seconds later without injury!

AND DID YOU KNOW...

- **Just in Case:** The Eisenhower interstate system requires that one mile in every five must be straight. These straight sections are usable as airstrips in times of war or other emergencies.

- **Blow Drying Satellites:** NASA scientists are still receiving data from Voyager even though the signal it is emitting has less energy than that emitted by a blow drier.

TRAIN TRACKS

The distance between train-track rails, better known as the U.S. Railroad gauge, is an odd 4 feet, 8.5 inches. Why? Because that's the way they built them in England, and English expatriates built the U.S. railroads.

But why did the English build them that size? Well, the first rail lines were built by those who built horse drawn tramways, and they simply used the same gauge. And they used that gauge because the people who built the tramways used the same jigs and tools used for building wagons—which use that wheel spacing.

But why did the wagons use that odd wheel spacing? If they tried to use any other spacing, the wagons wheels would break because they did not fit in the old ruts. So who built these old rutted roads? The first long-distance roads in Europe were built by Imperial Rome for the benefit of their legions. And the ruts? They were first made for Roman war chariots and they used the 4 feet, 8.5 inches measurement–they were all alike in the matter of wheel spacing.

But why that width? They were made to be just wide enough to accommodate the back-ends of two warhorses. *Alas, the influence of old ruts tends to live on forever. Many people are following ruts of theological tradition and have no idea where they started.*

AND DID YOU KNOW...

- **Jeep:** The name Jeep came from the abbreviation used in the army for the "General Purpose" vehicle, G.P.

- **Gas Guzzler:** The cruise liner Queen Elizabeth II moves only six inches for each gallon of diesel that it burns.

- **The Whole Nine Yards:** This comes from WWII fighter pilots in the South Pacific. Their .50 caliber machine gun ammo belts measured exactly 27 feet. If the pilots fired all their ammo at a target, it got "the whole 9 yards."

TYPEWRITER ARRANGEMENT

Credit for the first modern typewriter belongs to Christopher Sholes, a newspaper editor who lived in Milwaukee in the 1860s. On the Sholes model, as on present-day manual typewriters, each character was set on the end of a metal bar that struck the paper when its key was pressed. The keys were arranged alphabetically. But there was a snag—the bars attached to letters that lay close together on the keyboard became entangled with one another. One way out of the difficulty was to find out which letters were most often used in English, and then to re-site them on the keyboard as far from each other as possible.

This had the effect of reducing the chance of clashing type bars. In this way was born the QWERTY keyboard, named after the first six letters on the top line. Yet millions of modern computer keyboards are still using this cumbersome letter design.

AND DID YOU KNOW...

- **What?!** For a short time in 1967, the American Typers Association made a new punctuation mark that was a combination of the question mark and an exclamation point. They called it the interrobang. It was rarely used and hasn't been seen since.

- **Space Fender-Bender:** Only one satellite has been ever been destroyed by a meteor: the European Space Agency's Olympus in 1993.

- **Bock's Car:** The first atomic bomb dropped on Japan fell from the Enola Gay, named after the unit commander's mother. The second dropped from a plane known as Bock's Car.

USS NAUTILUS

Ancient explorers knew their exact location simply based on the sun, moon, and stars. Between 1768 and 1775, the famous British explorer James Cook made two voyages around the world, charting much of the South pacific, using nothing more than a sextant, a simple compass, and the heavens above for navigation.

For years, submarine navigation was a big problem. These secret vessels had to frequently surface to get their basic bearings, exposing themselves to enemy fire. But eventually, the U.S. Navy developed the internal marine gyro-navigation system. This sophisticated apparatus enabled subs to get a precise fix on their location even while isolated deep beneath the surface of a dark ocean.

This navigation system was fully proven in 1958 when the USS Nautilus accomplished the impossible. With 116 men on board, the nuclear-powered vessel became the first submarine to traverse the

Arctic Ocean under the polar ice. It traveled from the Bering Strait to Iceland via the North Pole in four days. Unable to surface, had the system failed, the crew would have been doomed.

In this world of constantly changing values we also need a dependable navigation system to guide our lives.

Psalm 48:14 *"For this God is our God for ever and ever: he will be our guide even unto death."*

THE QUEEN MARY

A floating city awash in elegance, the Queen Mary is one of the most famous ships in history. Launched in 1934 by Her Majesty Queen Mary, it was a wonder of modern times. The ship was considerably bigger than the infamous Titanic—with a 1,019-foot length and 12 decks reaching 181 feet high! The engines produced 160,000 horsepower to move the 81,000 gross tons! On August 30, 1934, the Queen Mary shattered a speed record by crossing the Atlantic in just under four days, averaging over 30 knots.

During its golden era, the Queen Mary boasted unprecedented luxury. Elegant kennels accommodated family pets and automobiles were stored in the hold. The ship's tailors would even redecorate a stateroom if the existing colors were not to one's liking.

The Queen Mary even played an epic role in World War II, transporting over 700,00 military personnel a total of 569,000 miles. In addition, she carried millions of passengers during her 1,001 voyages across the North Atlantic.

In 1967, the city of Long Beach bought the Queen Mary. Since then, $63 million has been spent on its conversion into a tourist spot with a museum, shops, restaurants, and hotel. *With no possibility of sailing the seas, the Queen Mary serves as false advertising—a ship filled with activity that never leaves port. This is like many modern churches—lots of history and activity, but is anybody going anywhere?*

SUNGLASSES

The first "sunglasses" were developed in China about A.D. 1430 using smoke to tint lenses. Ironically, the primary function of these blackened glasses was not to reduce solar glare or even vision correction! Instead, Chinese judges routinely wore them to conceal their eye expressions in court— their evaluation of evidence was credible only if it remained a secret until a trial's conclusion! Sunglasses are still worn by police to conceal their eyes from suspects while scrutinizing evidence. The Bible teaches that we have a heavenly judge who sees everything, including the thoughts of our hearts. We need to see Him clearly too!

The popularity of sunglasses is a 20th century phenomenon. In the 1930s, the Army Air Corps commissioned the optical firm Bausch & Lomb to produce a highly effective spectacle that would protect pilots from the dangers of glare when flying above clouds. The company opticians perfected a special dark-green tint that absorbed light in the spectrum's yellow band. They also designed a frame size to maximize the shielding of an aviator's eyes. Fliers were issued the ray-banning glasses at no charge, and soon the public was able to purchase these "Ray-Ban aviator sunglasses." A chic and clever 1960s' advertising campaign by Foster Grant made sunglasses a must have.

Psalm 139:23 "*Search me, O God, and know my heart: try me, and know my thoughts: And see if there be any wicked way in me, and lead me in the way everlasting.*"

AND DID YOU KNOW...

- **Jiffy Moment:** A "jiffy" is a unit of time: 3.3357 times 10 to the -11 (3.3357x10^-11) seconds. So named for the length of time it takes light to travel a centimeter in a vacuum.

- **Shaky Moment:** During the Manhattan Project in the early 1940s, the time it took for the imploding shell of plutonium to reach the center of the sphere was measured in "shakes of a lamb's tail." One shake = 1x10^-8 seconds. It took about three shakes of a lambs tail to get the uranium to a critical mass and initiate spontaneous fission.

INCA ROADS

Even without horses or wheeled vehicles to aid travel, a 12,000-mile network of Inca roads constituted a transportation network rivaled only by that of the Romans. It connected all parts of the realm, making possible swift communication; trained runners, working in relays, covered up to 250 miles per day.

AND DID YOU KNOW...

- **Short Hop:** The wingspan of a Boeing 747 jet is longer than the Wright Brothers' first flight.

- **Flying Railroad:** A railroad tanker car carrying propane traveled over 3,000 feet when it exploded during a train wreck in Illinois, sheering off a steel tower in its path. It's the longest flight on record for a propane explosion.

- **Brief, Brief Moment:** The smallest unit of time is the yoctosecond.

- **You're There:** The "you are here" arrow on maps is called an ideo locator.

ROMAN ROADS

At the height of its power, the Roman Empire had a road system of about 50,000 miles consisting of 29 highways radiating from the city of Rome. It helped them conquer the world. The Roman roads were four feet thick and consisted of three layers of successively finer stones set in mortar, with a layer of fitted stone blocks on top. By Roman law, the right of use of the roads belonged to all of the public, but the maintenance of the roadway was the responsibility of the inhabitants of the district through which the road ran.

MATCHES

For the first 5,800 years of history, if a man wanted to start a fire he had to rub two sticks together or make sparks with a flint and steel.

But in 1826, John Walker, an apothecary in England, was attempting to develop a new explosive in his lab. As he stirred this new mixture of chemicals, a drop of the substance dried on the end of the stirring stick. Then while cleaning the crusty lump off the stick, John wiped it on the floor and it suddenly ignited.

John made several of the friction matches to amuse and entertain friends but somehow missed their practical value. A man named Samuel Jones saw this demonstration and realized the commercial worth and went into a booming match business. Jones called his matches Lucifers. *It is worthy of mention that with the advent of phosphorus matches, tobacco smoking of all kinds greatly accelerated. Now we know where matches came from, but what about Satan? Did a loving God make the devil?*

AND DID YOU KNOW...

- **Big Steps:** The moon plaque placed by the crew of Apollo 11 reads: "Here men from the planet Earth first set foot upon the Moon July 1969, A.D. We came in peace for all mankind."

- **Khaki Camouflage:** The color Khaki was first used during the Afgahan War in 1880 because the color was considered good camouflage.

- **Always Golf to the Sunset:** Because of the Earths rotation an object can be thrown farther west.

- **Inflationary Travel:** It costs more to buy a new car in America today than it cost Christopher Columbus to equip and undertake three voyages to and from the New World.

- **Perfect 300:** A bowling pin need only tilt 7.5 degrees in order to fall down.

THE CHUNNEL

The idea of a tunnel under the English Channel connecting France with England began in the 18th century. But that seemingly impossible dream became reality in 1994.

The channel tunnel—or "Chunnel"—is in fact three tunnels, one service tunnel with two passenger tunnels on either side. The main tunnels are 25 feet in diameter and stretch 31 miles averaging 130 feet beneath the channel's seabed.

The Chunnel was constructed with 1,000-ton, laser-guided machines that dug 15 feet an hour as they also built retaining walls. These machines were so precise that after the first tunnel was completed, they were only a few centimeters off course.

The $13.5 billion, seven-year "Chunnel" is considered one of the wonders of the modern world. But a bigger marvel is a ladder that has been built reaching from heaven to earth!

1 Timothy 2:5 "For there is one God, and one mediator between God and men, the man Christ Jesus. ..."

ROLLER SKATES

The first practical pair of this wheeled phenomenon was called skaites and was built in 1759 by Belgian musical instrument maker Joseph Merlin. Each skate had only two wheels, aligned one in front of the other along the center of the shoe. The crude design was based on the ice skates of Merlin's day, which were strapped to the shoes.

Merlin constructed the skates to make a spectacular entrance at a costume party. A master violinist, he intended to roll into the party while playing his instrument. Unfortunately, he had neglected to master the fine art of stopping on skates—and when the big moment came, he careened through the room and crashed into a full-length mirror, breaking it and his violin; his entrance was indeed spectacular!

Did you know that in the near future, the devil is planning to make a spectacular appearance masquerading as Jesus Christ? But unlike Joseph Merlin, Satan has been practicing his dramatic entrance for 6,000 years!

AND DID YOU KNOW...

- **Worth It's Own Weight:** In English, "four" is the only number that has the same number of letters as its value.
- **Paper Facts:** No piece of square, dry paper can be folded more than 7 times in half.
- **Brick Counting:** There are more than 10 million bricks in the Empire State Building.

THE GORDIAN KNOT

Gordius was a Greek peasant who became king of Phrygia—because he was the first man to drive into town after an oracle had commanded his countrymen to select as ruler the first person who would drive into the public square in a wagon!

In gratitude, Gordius dedicated his wagon to the god Zeus and tied the tongue of the wagon securely in the temple grove with a thick strong rope. The knot was so intricately entwined that no one could undo it. Many tried, but all failed. A prophet said that whoever succeeded in untying the difficult knot would become the ruler of all Asia. Hearing this, Alexander the Great unsuccessfully attempted to untie the complex Gordian knot, so he drew his sword and cut it through with a single stroke. Alexander, of course, went on to become the ruler of Asia and beyond. The expression "to cut the Gordian knot" is now used for resolving a difficult problem by a quick and decisive action.

AND DID YOU KNOW...

- **If You're Bored:** If you counted 24 hours a day, it would take 31,688 years to reach one trillion.

- **Glazed Pennies:** The Mint once considered producing doughnut-shaped coins.

- **Irish Rebellion:** Windmills always turn counter-clockwise, except in Ireland.

- **Not Appreciated:** The Mayflower, after outliving its usefulness, was dismantled and rebuilt as a barn.

- **Big Computer, Small Computing:** The first electronic computer was about 80 feet long, weighed 30 tons, and had 17,000 tubes.

- **Groovy Facts:** A quarter has 119 grooves on its edge, a dime has one less groove!

- **Heavy Home:** The planet earth is estimated to weigh around 6,600,000,000,000,000,000,000 tons (5,940 billion billion metric tons)!

- **Shoe, Shoe:** The plastic on the end of a shoelace is called an *aglet*.

CANNED FOOD

When Napoleon's armies invaded Europe, his generals soon realized that an "army marches on its stomach," and that foraging for food was wasting time. But when the armies tried to carry their food with them, it spoiled. So in 1795, the French government offered a prize of 12,000 francs to any Frenchman who could find a way to preserve food. Yet it wasn't until 1809 that a French confectioner named Nicholas Appert claimed the money.

After years of experiment, Appert placed peas and carrots into wine bottles, cooked them at a high temperature, and then sealed the glass with a cork. The food remained edible after standing many days, and thus was discovered the basic principle of modern canning. Food preservation techniques have become so sophisticated that perishables can be preserved and remain edible for centuries. *Perhaps you would be interested to know what is the most perishable food in history? And Moses said, "Let no one leave any of it till morning." Notwithstanding they did not heed Moses. But some of them left part of it until morning, and it bred worms and stank. And Moses was angry with them. So they gathered it every morning, every man according to his need. And when the sun became hot, it melted (**Exodus 16:19–21**).*

CANAL DU MIDI

A 60-year-old man of genius, Pierre-Paul de Riquet began the grandest project of his life when most his age are thinking retirement. In the 17th century, the intrepid French engineer conceived the idea of constructing a canal across France from the Mediterranean to the Atlantic. Since the government refused to share the cost of the gigantic enterprise, old Pierre decided to assume the enormous project himself.

Riquet's design called for a canal that traveled uphill to a point and then downhill the other way, like crossing a bridge, whereas most canals of the day simply descended. This design would serve to save time and help ships avoid pirates lurking along the straits of Gibraltar, and it would join the economies of the Mediterranean to the Atlantic. With nothing more than shovels and primitive tools, 12,000 laborers worked 14 years from 1666 to 1681 to create the incredibly long trench.

During its construction, Pierre-Paul Riquet oversaw the entire project. The 79-foot wide passageway with its 8-foot depth, its 228 bridges and 114 locks, gradually lifted water 621 feet and then back down to the level of the Atlantic. This feat beckoned the amazement and the admiration of all Europe. King Louis XIV referred to it as the greatest achievement of his entire 72-year reign. The 158-mile Canal du Midi (or middle canal) is an engineering marvel and the oldest functioning canal in Europe. It has been of immeasurable benefit to the French people since the day it was built, even aiding Napoleon in his conquest of Europe.

This purely civil project was paid for by the money of one man—that's right: 158 miles costing $68 million. It came from his fortune he had earned as the salt-tax collector. He sacrificed everything to ensure the canal's completion—even using his wife's fortune and his daughters' dowries for the cause.

Sadly, six months before its completion, Riquet, exhausted and sick, retired in his home and died without ever seeing his life's masterpiece achieved. *The Bible tells us about someone else who personally paid a king's ransom to provide a conduit for us.*

1 Corinthians 6:20 "*For ye are bought with a price: therefore glorify God in your body, and in your spirit, which are God's.*"

Contents:

GEORGE WASHINGTON CARVER

Born of slave parents in Diamond Grove, Missouri, Carver was rescued from Confederate kidnappers as an infant. He began his education in Newton County in southwest Missouri, where he worked as a farmhand and studied in a one-room schoolhouse. He is perhaps the nation's best-known African-American scientist. In the period between 1890 and 1910, the cotton crop had been devastated by the boll weevil. Carver advised to cultivate peanuts, and before long, he developed more than 300 different peanut-based products—everything from milk to printer's ink. At Tuskegee, Carver developed his crop rotation method, which alternated nitrate-producing legumes—such as peanuts and peas—with cotton, which depletes soil of its nutrients. Following Carver's lead, southern farmers soon began planting peanuts one year and cotton the next. While many of the peanuts were used to feed livestock, large surpluses quickly developed. When he discovered that the sweet potato and the pecan also enriched depleted soils, Carver found almost 20 uses for these crops, including synthetic rubber and material for paving highways.

BEING BOLD-TELEMACHUS

Around A.D. 400, the great Coliseum in Rome was often packed as spectators watched the violent games in which human beings battled one another or wild beasts until one was killed. People reveled in such sport and found their highest delight when a person was slain. On one such a day, a Syrian monk named Telemachus stood up. He was grieved and outraged by the utter disregard for human life and leaped into the arena in the midst of the carnage! He boldly cried out, "This thing is not right! This thing must stop!" Because he was interfering with their entertainment, the authorities commanded for Telemachus to be run through with a sword. But his death kindled a flame in the hearts and consciences of many. History tells us that because of his courageous sacrifice, within a few months these blood baths began to decline and soon ended.

Acts 22:15 "For thou shalt be his witness unto all men of what thou hast seen and heard."

DAVID ATCHISON

One U.S. President slept through his entire term of office! He was David Rice Atchison, but you probably haven't heard of him— very few have. But Senator Atchison did serve as President. Here's how it happened:

James Polk's term as the 11th U.S. President expired on Saturday, March 3, 1849. President-elect Zachary Taylor did not want to be inaugurated on a Sunday; he preferred the ceremonies to be held on Monday, March 5. Yet the United States could not be without a leader, even for 24 hours, so the next person in line was President Pro-tem of the Senate, who happened to be Senator David Rice Atchison. He, therefore, took over the office for that Sunday.

Atchison later explained his "sleeping term" by saying that his last day of work in congress was so heavy and busy that he went to bed very late Saturday night exhausted. He slept soundly, even snoring, all through the day that he was President—-March 4, 1849. How sad to be President for a day and not remember a single minute!

The Bible also teaches that during some of the most important and crucial moments, God's people have gone to sleep.

Matthew 26:39-41 "And he went a little farther, and fell on his face, *and prayed, saying, O my Father, if it be possible, let this cup pass from me: nevertheless not as I will, but as thou wilt. And he cometh unto the disciples, and findeth them asleep, and saith unto Peter, What, could ye not watch with me one hour? Watch and pray, that ye enter not into temptation: the spirit indeed is willing, but the flesh is weak."*

DAVID HANNUM

In upstate New York, George Hull and his cousin William Newell plotted to bamboozle the public. They hired a Chicago sculptor to carve a fake, 10-foot prehistoric man from a 3,000-pound hunk of gypsum. Then they arranged for well drillers to "find" the fake fossil, which they had buried on their farm. The Cardiff Giant, as it became known, soon became a popular attraction, enticing crowds to pay 50 cents to see the "petrified remains." The carving looked so authentic that scientists argued whether the Cardiff Giant was a real petrified man or a prehistoric statue.

Newell eventually sold the giant to banker David Hannum, who displayed it in Syracuse. He charged a dollar per person to see it—a fantastic amount in 1869. Meanwhile, P. T. Barnum was looking for a new exhibit for his American Museum, which was famous for such oddities as the White Whale, the Fiji Mermaid (the upper half of a monkey joined to a fishtail), and the famous dwarf General Tom Thumb. He even exhibited a former slave woman named Joice Heth, who claimed to be the 161-year-old childhood nurse of George Washington.

Barnum offered Hannum $60,000 for the Cardiff giant, but Hannum refused. So the ever-resourceful Barnum just made a copy, which he called the original. Hannum applied for a court order to stop Barnum, but the judge ruled that both men had fake giants and reasoned that a forgery of a fraud was no crime. When the disgruntled Hannum saw the crowds lining up to see Barnum's copy, he said, "There's a sucker born every minute."

With all the swindles, scams and cons in the world today, people everywhere are wondering if there is anywhere they can go for dependable truth?

Psalm 25:5 *"Lead me in thy truth, and teach me: for thou art the God of my salvation; on thee do I wait all the day."*

ALEXANDER SELKIRK

Daniel Defoe's famous novel *Robinson Crusoe* is the adventurous story of one man's courage and ability to survive the ultimate tests of nature alone on an uninhabited island. Yet few people know that Robinson Crusoe really did exist, but his real name was Alexander Selkirk. Daniel Defoe based his novel on Selkirk's real-life adventure.

Selkirk was born in 1676 in Largo, Scotland. This son of a tanner was an adventurer at heart, so he ran away in 1695 for the sea and eventually joined William Dampier on an expedition plundering Spanish merchant ships. In September of 1704, after a serious quarrel with Captain Dampier, the hotheaded Selkirk requested that he be put ashore on the uninhabited island of Juan Fernandez, 400 miles west of Chile. (It was fortunate for Selkirk, because Dampier's ship later sank and most of the crew was lost.)

Selkirk's possessions included his clothes, bedding, a flintlock, gunpowder, bullets, a hatchet, a knife, a kettle, and a Bible. He stayed busy but for the first eight months, but had to bear up against melancholy and the terror of being left alone in such a desolate place. He built two huts from pimento trees, covered with long grass, and lined them with the skins of goats, which were abundant on the island. He also made himself clothes with goat skins. When his gunpowder was spent, he created fire by rubbing two sticks together.

Great numbers of cats and rats plagued his island life. He eventually tamed many of the cats, and they would lie about in hundreds and delivered him from the rats. To divert himself, he sang and danced with goats and cats. In time, he conquered all the inconveniences of his solitude and found happiness on the island.

Selkirk remained alone on the island for more than four years. Finally, in February 1709, Captain Woodes Rogers discovered him while sailing the ship Duke, whose pilot happened to be old Captain Dampier. Despite his long castaway, Selkirk was given command of a captured Spanish ship. Selkirk returned to England in 1711, and his story was published. A few years later, *Robinson Crusoe* appeared. Selkirk finally returned home to Scotland, living as a recluse, but he later returned to the sea where he died in 1721.

Someone once said "No man is an island," and the Bible says it is not good for a man to be alone. But does this mean it is God's will for everybody to be married?

AND DID YOU KNOW...

- **Patriotic Procrastination:** Only two people signed the Declaration of Independence on July 4: John Hancock and Charles Thomson. Most of the rest signed on August 2, but the last signature wasn't added until 5 years later.

- **Women of Invention:** Bullet proof vests, fire escapes, windshield wipers and laser printers were all invented by women.

- **When the Last Aren't the First:** While almost everyone knows that Neil Armstrong was the first man to walk on the moon, few know that Gene Cernan was the last.

ALFRED NOBEL

You've probably heard of the Nobel Peace Prize, but what about the strange history behind the prestigious award?

Alfred Nobel was born in 1833 in Stockholm, Sweden. He received a good education in Russia and soon took a job as a chemical engineer. Though Alfred Nobel did not invent nitroglycerin, he was the first to produce it commercially. In 1863, he developed a detonator that relied on strong shock rather than heat. But Nitroglycerin in its fluid state is very volatile, and in 1864, an explosion killed his brother Emil and several others. Recognizing this danger, Nobel moved his lab and soon invented dynamite, also known as "Nobel's safety blasting powder."

This new material, nitro, absorbed by a porous clay substance, was five times more powerful than gunpowder and provided an easily handled, solid yet malleable explosive. Mining, railroad building, and other construction became much safer, more efficient, and cheaper. But military leaders soon realized the wartime value of dynamite.

This deadly use of his creation greatly troubled the "Lord of Dynamite," a pacifist, and strongly opposed the wartime uses of his inventions. Yet Nobel continued to produce nitroglycerin-based explosives, saying he was producing weapons so powerful that no one would dare use them. (So much for that theory!) Alfred was also a great entrepreneur—he founded 90 factories and laboratories in more than 20 countries and held 355 patents in his lifetime.

In 1895, a newspaper confused the death of Alfred's older brother with him, and published Alfred's obituary! Nobel read it and was horrified that he would be remembered as the man who created the explosive that caused so much carnage. Perhaps to alleviate his conscience and improve his legacy, his will provided that at his death, the bulk of his vast fortune should go to a fund that awards prizes for advancements in science, medicine, literature, and peace.

Few people read their obituary before their death and fewer still get a chance to change their reputation. But because of the matchless gift and sacrifice of Jesus we can have a new name.

Revelation 2:17 "He that hath an ear, let him hear what the Spirit saith unto the churches; To him that overcometh will I give to eat of the hidden manna, and will give him a white stone, and in the stone a new name written, which no man knoweth saving he that receiveth it."

DESMOND T. DOSS

After being drafted, Desmond Doss' refusal to bear arms gave his commanders fits, and his fellow soldiers used this meek misfit as a punching bag. His faith (Seventh-day Adventist) forbade the taking of lives and promoted their saving. He always kept his Bible close by but refused to carry a weapon at his own peril. Yet as an infantry medic during World War II, Doss did as much as any great warrior to save the lives of his fellow men.

During a bloody assault in Okinawa in late April 1945, private first-class Doss exhibited magnificent fortitude and unflinching bravery in the face of dangerous conditions. He retrieved 75 wounded men off a rocky cliff while under constant enemy fire. Doss believed this impressive feat was made possible only by the guiding and protective hand of God. Doss received many wounds during that battle and others, but he always tended to others before himself.

His reputation as a soldier propelled his name as a symbol for outstanding faith and gallantry far above and beyond the call of duty throughout the 77th Infantry Division. While seriously wounded after jumping on a grenade to protect his fellow men, Doss dragged himself through the battlefield to treat wounded soldiers until he was rescued. Doss later discovered he'd lost his Bible during the conflict. However, the respect of his fellow soldiers had grown so profound that they searched the battlefield until they found the beloved Book of the private they had all once mocked. For his heroic efforts and bravery, Doss received this country's highest honor. On Columbus Day in 1945, President Truman placed the Congressional Medal of Honor around Doss' neck and said, "This is a greater honor for me than being president." This made Doss the only conscientious objector to ever receive the award.

AND DID YOU KNOW...

- **Huddle Up:** The football huddle originated at Gallaudet University, the world's only accredited four-year liberal arts college for the deaf. It was started in the 19th century, when the football team found that opposing teams were reading their signed messages and intercepting plays.

- **Already Short:** The shortest British monarch was Charles I, who was 4'9"—and that was before he lost his head!

- **It's Up to the Canadians:** Since World War II, every American president to address the Canadian House of Commons in their first term of office have all been re-elected to a second term. Eisenhower, Nixon, Reagan, and Clinton have all had the honor, while Kennedy, Johnson, Ford, Carter, and Bush did not address the parliament.

CHENG HO

Born in the Chinese province of Yunnan in 1371, Ma Sanpao (Cheng Ho) was captured and sent to serve in the army under Chu Ti in 1382. There he helped Chu Ti become Emperor Yonglo of the Ming Dynasty. To reward his work, Ma was made Grand Imperial Eunuch—and his name was changed to Zheng He.

Yonglo chose Zheng to head a series of naval expeditions to ports all over the Indian Ocean. Zheng had diplomatic, scientific, and commercial goals while traveling farther than any other admiral in history. He visited more than 35 countries, utilizing more than 100 ships and nearly 28,000 men in his Grand Fleet. The largest vessels were 444-foot treasure ships!

The fleet visited southern Asia in the first voyage and by the seventh and last voyage, Zheng had been to east Africa, the Persian Gulf, Egypt and Ceylon (modern day Sri Lanka). Almost 30 countries sent envoys back to China to give homage to the emperor, and each nation eagerly welcomed Zheng and traded for Chinese goods. He set up diplomatic relations in each country he visited and received tribute from most rulers.

In Ceylon, Zheng helped restore the legitimate ruler to the throne. In Indonesia, the fleet defeated a powerful Chinese pirate. Zheng's voyages not only established Chinese trade routes throughout Asia and Africa, but also established China as the dominant world power. China was far more technologically advanced than any other culture, and no European force could have successfully challenged its authority.

Emperor Yonglo died in 1424, ending all naval expeditions until 1431. Between two and five years after Yonglo's death, Cheng Ho himself died during a trip home from India, ending the seventh and final voyage of the Grand Fleet. China eventually banned all naval expeditions indefinitely. Future emperors practiced strict isolationism and burned all records of Cheng Ho's voyages. Chinese influence on the world ended and opened the door for the rise of European superpowers.

KING TUT

Tutankhamen is probably the most famous Egyptian pharaoh and is better known as King Tut. This boy king died in his late teens and remained at rest for more than 3,300 years. But that changed in 1922 when Egyptologist Howard Carter, who was excavating in the Valley of the Kings, discovered the king's tomb.

Still, it came close to escaping discovery altogether! Carter had been searching for the tomb for a number of years on behalf of English patron, Lord Carnarvon, who later decided that enough time and money had been expended with little return. However, Carter managed to persuade his patron to fund one more season, and within days of resuming excavation, the missing tomb was found full of treasures.

Today, the tomb still contains the pharaoh's remains, hidden from view inside the outermost of three coffins. He is believed to be the only pharaoh still residing in the Valley of the Kings.

King Tut's tomb has yielded some of the greatest treasures of antiquity, but the most priceless treasure of all time is actually in an empty tomb outside Jerusalem!

AND DID YOU KNOW...

- **Moving Library:** Abdul Kassem Ismael, Grand Vizier of Persia in the 10th century, carried his library with him wherever he went. The 117,000 volumes were carried by 400 camels trained to walk in alphabetical order.

- **Patriotic Sobriety:** The music for the Star Spangled Banner is from an old British drinking song. Francis Scott Key, writer of the Star Spangled Banner, was a lawyer.

- **Mirror Image:** The Dutch painter Rembrandt, often called the master of light and shade, painted almost 100 self-portraits.

THOMAS PARR

Westminster Abbey in London is one of Great Britain's most-famous churches. This splendid edifice was built in stages beginning in the 11th century, and it enshrines many of the traditions of the British people.

English monarchs since William the Conqueror have been crowned in the abbey, and most are buried in its chapels. Famous citizens like Isaac Newton and David Livingstone are also buried there. But one of the most amazing people buried in the Abby is a farmer named Thomas Parr.

Born in 1483 during the reign of King Richard III, Parr is believed to have lived to the age of 152, witnessing the seating of 10 sovereigns on the throne during his long life—including the 50-year reign of Queen Elizabeth I.

In 1635, King Charles I invited Thomas Parr to the palace that he might meet this remarkable man. The king inquired as to what Thomas owed his long life? He answered that he lived a simple life, eating mostly potatoes and oatmeal. While at the palace, old Thomas feasted on the rich food served at the palace. He was not used to this food, and that night after dining on the king's delicacies, he became very ill and died. King Charles felt so terrible having killed Britain's oldest citizen with his food that he commanded Parr to be buried in Westminster Abbey.

Did you know that the Bible tells of another man who refused to eat a king's food and lived a long life?

WINSTON CHURCHILL

A wealthy family in England took their children to the country where they went swimming. When one of their boys began to drown, the son of a local gardener bravely jumped in to rescue him. The parents were so grateful for this deed, they asked the gardener what they could do for the young hero. The gardener said that his son desperately wanted to go to college to become a doctor, but he could not afford the tuition. The Churchill family gladly agreed to pay the courageous boy's way through school for saving their son Winston.

Years later, after the Teheran Conference, Winston Churchill was stricken with pneumonia. The King of England instructed that the best doctor be found to save the gravely ill Prime Minister. The doctor chosen was Sir Alexander Fleming, the developer of penicillin and Nobel laureate, who nursed Winston Churchill back to health. "Rarely," said Churchill to Fleming, "has one man owed his life twice to the same rescuer." It was Fleming who had saved Churchill from drowning in that pool in his youth.

THE LADY WHO GREW BACKWARD

The "Lady Who Grew Backward" was a woman who lived in Virginia some years ago. In the Virginia Medical Monthly her doctor told her story:

She had grown normally, married and had three children. Life was happy, until her husband and father died when the children were in high school. The mother doubled her devotion to her children, changing her clothes to those of a 20 year old and joined in her children's activities.

In a few years, the children noticed that as they grew older, their mother grew younger. Psychiatrists call this "personality regression," which literally means "a person walking backward." Usually, such people stop going backward at a certain age, but not this woman. She slipped backward at the rate of one year for every three to four months. Although she was 61 years old, she acted and spoke like a six year old. She was sent to a sanitarium, where she insisted on wearing short dresses, playing with toys and babbling like a child.

Soon she became like a three-year-old; she spilled her food, crawled on the floor and cried "mama." Backward still further to the age of one, she drank milk and curled up like a baby. Finally, she crossed the line and died.

Revelation 22:3-5, 7 "And there shall be no more curse: but the throne of God and of the Lamb shall be in it; and his servants shall serve him: And they shall see his face; and his name shall be in their foreheads. And there shall be no night there; and they need no candle, neither light of the sun; for the Lord God giveth them light: and they shall reign for ever and ever... Behold, I come quickly: blessed is he that keepeth the sayings of the prophecy of this book."

MIHAILO TOLOTOS

This is probably the only healthy man in modern history who never saw the form or heard the voice of a woman! The monk Mihailo died in 1938 at the age of 82 in one of the monasteries atop Mount Athos in Greece. When his mother passed away during his birth, Mihailo was taken to Athos. Not once in his entire life did he leave this monastic colony, which for more than 900 years has strictly excluded all females—both animal and human.

EARL OF WILTSHIRE

At odds with Pope Clement VII for refusing to annul his marriage to Catherine of Aragón, King Henry VIII sent a delegation to the Vatican in an effort to patch up the political differences between himself and the Pope. The Earl of Wiltshire led the delegation—he also took his dog.

As was customary, the Earl prostrated himself before the Pope and was about to kiss the pontiff's toe. The Pope, always willing to receive the homage, thrust his foot toward the Earl, but the Earl's watching dog mistook the action and went to defend his master. Instead of a kiss, the Pope received a bite on the toe!

This so enraged the Swiss Guard that they instantly killed the poor dog. Terribly angered, the Earl stormed away and refused to proceed with the mission to reconcile England with Rome. After the Earl's return, King Henry took permanent steps to separate the Church of England from the jurisdiction of Rome. The Anglican Church was born.

KING HUMBERT

Naples was on the verge of insurrection against the Italian monarchy when King Humbert took the throne. Politicians urged violent measures to force the city into submission, but King Humbert refused. However, Naples was soon hit by an outbreak of cholera, and the dreaded disease raged with deadly fury.

Ignoring his advisors, the young king, moved with devotion for even his disloyal subjects, left the palace and went alone through the crowded hospitals of Naples, ministering to his subjects. Many of the suffering breathed prayers of gratitude for this young medical servant, not knowing it was the very king they'd spurned. When the plague was finally checked, many learned his true identity. Naples then became a conquered city—conquered by the love of a monarch it once refused. From that time forward, the people of Naples were among Humbert's most loyal subjects.

Matthew 4:23 *"And Jesus went about all Galilee, teaching in their synagogues, and preaching the gospel of the kingdom, and healing all manner of sickness and all manner of disease among the people."*

NAVAJO CODE TALKERS

During the Pacific battles of World War II, the Japanese eavesdropped on U.S. Marine communications and managed to decipher the coded messages. In fact, Japanese cryptographers succeeded in breaking every U.S. code as fast as it was developed. But there was one code they could never break.

The idea originated with Philip Johnston, an engineer and World War I veteran, who knew of the military's need for an unbreakable code. He was raised on a Navajo Reservation where his father had been a missionary. Navajo was virtually an unwritten language in 1942, with no alphabet or symbols, and was spoken only on the Navajo lands of the American Southwest.

Confident that few people in the world understood the complex syntax and tonal qualities of Navajo, Johnston suggested that the army use the language as the basis for code. After staging an impressive demonstration in which several Navajo friends transmitted English into Navajo and back to English, the Marines authorized an official program to develop and implement the code.

Twenty-nine Navajos fluent in their native tongue and English, some only 15 years old, constructed and mastered the Navajo code, which they used to transmit crucial information in battles. More were trained later. Historians believe that the Navajo code talkers played a fundamental role in the U.S. victory in the Pacific.

Did you know the Scriptures teach there is a little known code that once understood will unlock the mysteries of Bible prophecy?

CHARLES GRANDEMANGE

Perhaps the strangest human computer, Charles Grandemange of France was born in 1835—a mere one-pound baby. Yet he was endowed with a prodigious brain. At age 14, he toured Europe in demonstration of his calculating ability. He lived in a wooden box only one foot wide, but he could multiply two 100-digit numbers by one another within thirty seconds. He could divide a 23-digit figure by another and find the remainder at one glance. He was billed as the fastest of all lightning calculators.

AND DID YOU KNOW...

- **Humble President:** President Grover Cleveland had the first telephone installed in the White House in the late 1880s. He always answered the phone himself.
- **Smart Guy:** Thomas Edison held over 1,300 U.S. and foreign patents.
- **Hold Hands in the Extreme:** Hands Across America took place in 1986. It was 4,150 miles long.

FREE FALLERS

Believe it or not, in January 1942, Russian Lieutenant Chisov survived a 22,000-foot fall without a parachute from his badly damaged plane. He providentially fell on the edge of a ravine covered with snow and, because he struck it glancingly, slid as he landed. He was badly injured but survived to return to his duties.

An even more incredible escape happened to U.S. Flight Sergeant Alkemade in 1944, when he jumped from his blazing bomber over Germany, also without a parachute. He fell headlong 18,000 feet, but a fir tree broke the fall as he continued downwards into a knee-high bank of snow. The damage? None!

On July 9, 1960, Roger Woodard became the first person known to survive a plunge over the Niagara Falls without a barrel. He and a friend were boating above the falls when the motor failed. A huge wave overturned the boat, throwing both into the swift current. Roger's companion vanished, while he, wearing a life jacket, was swept over the 162-foot precipice.

The tourist boat, *Maid of the Mist*, happened to be at the bottom of the falls and the captain heard Roger crying "Help!" A year later, Woodard accepted Christ as his Savior, and said: "I guess the Lord saved me the first time so that I could be saved the second time."

HAROLD WEST

When Harold West died, his doctor drove a stake through his heart to make sure he was dead. When he was buried, they did not nail his coffin shut just in case he was not completely dead. But West was no vampire; he was just an over-cautious banker who deathly feared to be buried alive. When West died at 90, he left a will directing that "my coffin shall not be screwed down and that a surgeon be instructed to pierce my heart with a steel or other instrument to make certain death has occurred."

For years, Christian critics have said the resurrection never happened because Jesus was not actually dead when they buried Him, but rather in a comatose state from which he revived. Sadly, now some pastors are saying that Jesus was not really dead in the tomb, but that He entered a different realm to preach to the lost from past ages.

DR. WELCH

In 1869, Dr. Thomas Bramwell Welch, a physician and dentist by profession, successfully pasteurized Concord grape juice to produce an "unfermented sacramental wine" for fellow parishioners at his church in Vineland, New Jersey. He was inspired to do this after a visitor became drunk and unruly following a communion service in which fermented wine was used. Since antiquity, there have been several methods of preserving wine from fermenting, but they always sacrificed much in the way of taste. Dr. Welch's process preserved both. Today, Welch's Grape juice is an international food company.

ALEXANDER THE GREAT

Alexander the Great was ruler of Macedonia at age 16, a victorious general at 18, and king at 20—he then died from alcohol before age 33. The story:

After Alexander began a second night of carousing in Babylon with 20 guests at table, he drank to the health of every person at the table. For Proteas, a Macedonian in his company, Alexander called for Hercules' cup, which had a huge capacity. After filling it, he drank it all down. Soon he fell to the floor, was fever-stricken, and—a few days later—dead. He had conquered the then-known world, but not himself.

Proverbs 20:1 "*Wine is a mocker, strong drink is raging: and whosoever is deceived thereby is not wise.*"

ELVIS

Born in a modest, two-bedroom house, Elvis Presley would become the most famous entertainer in the world. He sold so many albums that you could place each of them side by side at the equator and circle the globe four times.

With strong Christian roots, Elvis often quoted his favorite book, the Bible. His favorite verse was *1 Corinthians 13:1*. But Elvis' meteoric rise to fame was far less remarkable than his ultimate plummet into darkness.

The once energetic, healthy Presley suffered a drug-related cardiac arrest at his home in Memphis, where over-eating, drug-use, and other self-abuses were rampant. When he died, Elvis had earned nearly $250 million, but his estate was valued at less than $10 million. Another famous verse that supposedly haunted him later in life is *Matthew 19:24.*

His extravagant, idolized lifestyle is still celebrated today. Elvis Presley Enterprises Inc. makes more than $50 million a year from licensing the "King's" image alone.

POMP AND POLO

Marco Polo reports that the Great Kublai Khan of China was enormously respected. Anybody coming within 500 meters from him had to lower his voice and behave humbly. If someone had an invitation to the palace, he had to take off his shoes and put on white leather slippers before entering the palace. If he wished to spit, he had to take with him a small covered vessel. Forgetting to respect the Great Khan could quickly result in death from the hands of one of his 10,000 bodyguards!

MICHEL LOTITO

This Frenchman has a very unusual diet. Born on June 15, 1950, he has been consuming large quantities of metal and glass since he was nine years old. To date, he has eaten supermarket carts, television sets, bicycles, chandeliers, razor blades, bullets, nuts and bolts, lengths of chain, phonograph records, computers, and an entire Cessna 150 light aircraft (which took him nearly two years to consume). It seems that his body has adjusted to this unusual diet, as he eats nearly two pounds of metal every day. His technique includes lubricating his digestive tract with mineral oil, cutting the parts into bite-size pieces, and then consuming a large quantity of water while eating this junk. *Source: Reader's Digest Facts & Fallacies, 1988, Reader's Digest*

DAVID DOUGLAS

In 1825, David Douglas sailed along the west coast of the United States and up the Columbia River. Only 26-years-old, the young botanist from London was on a quest—a lifelong dream: Study the New World's plant life. Since a boy, Douglas had been obsessed with plants, and by the age of 21, he was appointed to the Royal Botanical Gardens in Scotland.

As the ship approached land, one particular tree captivated David. As he reported, "So pleased was I that I could scarcely see [anything] but it." He couldn't wait to see the tree up close, and when he did, he pronounced it "one of the most striking and truly graceful objects in nature." It was only fitting that this famous tree would later bear his name—the Douglas fir.

David spent the next two years exploring the Northwest, finding new plants and shipping more than 500 species back to England. William Hooker, one of the world's leading botanists, described David as a man of "great activity, undaunted courage, ... and energetic zeal." The Native Americans were immensely impressed with David's endurance, but they also questioned his sanity. They called him "Man of Grass," because he would hike from first dawn to dusk collecting plants that he couldn't eat! His collecting adventures took him 12,000 miles on foot, horseback, and canoe. There are more plants named for Douglas, over 200, than for any other person in the history of science.

On an 1829 trip to North America, Douglas made a discovery that eventually changed the history of the New World. While collecting specimens in California, he pulled a plant from the ground that contained flecks of gold, which clung to the roots. But as David packed the plant for shipment, he saw only the plant. That's how gold was first discovered in California in 1831—not by loggers in Sutter creek, but by the botanists in London who unpacked David's shipment of plants and saw gold on the roots.

David Douglas had only one purpose in life. Nothing, not even gold, could distract him from his mission. And this mission was well established by the time he was 11 years of age. *That is the sort of focused energetic zeal that God wants from us today!*

1 Timothy 6:12 "Fight the good fight of faith, lay hold on eternal life, whereunto thou art also called, and hast professed a good profession before many witnesses."

NAVY SEALS

During the Gulf War, a small team of U.S. Navy SEALS created a diversion so convincing that it completely fooled the Iraqi army. About a dozen SEALS stormed the beaches of Kuwait and created such havoc that Iraqi generals believed the U.S.-led attack was coming from the sea. Iraq sent the majority of their army to repel this fake attack—only to find they had been duped as the main U.S. force came through the Saudi Arabian desert! Within hours the war was over, and it all started with less than 20 soldiers!

Of course, each branch of the U.S. armed services has one or more elite teams of commandos that fight using covert guerrilla warfare tactics during special combat situations. To serve in one of these select units, a soldier must be highly disciplined and pass through incredibly difficult physical and mental training. Only those who demonstrate unflinching self control and perfect obedience qualify. These special forces commandos are given dangerous and complex missions; they rapidly attack enemy troops and raid behind enemy lines to clear the way for the main attacking force. Even a small team of these commandos, because of their intense training, can achieve great victories—defeating entire columns in short time.

The book of Revelation tells us of another special forces unit—a vast "army" of 144,000. They are commissioned with the greatest mission in the last days: prepare the world for Jesus' return.

AND DID YOU KNOW...

- **Assassin Facts:** John Wilkes Booth shot Lincoln in a theatre and was found in a warehouse. Lee Harvey Oswald shot Kennedy from a warehouse and was found in a theatre.

- **Franz Ferdinand:** The death of this archbishop partly caused World War I. But his death was almost unavoidable. After an attempted assassination with a bomb failed, (because the bomb hit the rear mud flap of the car Ferdinand was in and bounced away) authorities decided to change the route of Ferdinand's tour—but failed to inform the driver of the car. And so, unfortunately, the driver took a wrong turn and drove into an alley. While reversing out, Princip jumped out and shot Ferdinand and his wife, killing them. Ferdinand had simply brought his wife to Sarajevo to celebrate their anniversary.

- **Rosalind Franklin:** The woman behind Watson and Crick's double helix DNA model was Rosalind Franklin. She did all the experiments, but died before she was paid credit. Watson and Crick merely took her results and interpreted it.

  Psalm 9:1-2 "*I will praise thee, O LORD, with my whole heart; I will show forth all thy marvellous works. I will be glad and rejoice in thee: I will sing praise to thy name, O thou Most High.*"

THE REAL ST. PATRICK

Typically on March 17, people all over the world join with the Irish to celebrate Saint Patrick's Day. Cities like New York and Boston have large parades baptized in shamrocks, leprechauns, and green. Chicago even dyes its river green!

But sadly, there is far more myth than fact taught about this great man of God. For starters, this patron saint of Ireland wasn't even Irish, but Scottish. St. Patrick was born Maewyn Succat in Roman Britain around A.D. 389. He was captured by raiders when he was 16 and shipped to Ireland, where he was sold as a slave caring for pigs and sheep. While in captivity, he surrendered his heart to Christ. After six years, he escaped back to his homeland. But later, he distinctly heard God call him to return to Ireland as a missionary to convert his captors. After he became a minister, he took on the name Patrick or Patricus, which means "father of the people."

A popular legend has it that St. Patrick drove all the snakes from Ireland. It's true, that aside from zoos, there are no snakes on the Emerald Isle. But that's because there never were any snakes in Ireland! This tale might have arisen as a metaphor of his single-handed effort to drive the idol-worshiping Druid cult out of Ireland. When Patrick began his mission about 430, Ireland was gripped by paganism and idolatry. Druid priests practiced spiritism, black magic and performed human sacrifices to appease the local gods. It is also rumored, and not confirmed, that he used a shamrock not as a good luck charm, but as a simple illustration to explain the Trinity.

Saint Patrick was not technically a saint because the Catholic Church never canonized him. Fantastic as it might seem, even though they built hundreds of churches that bare his name, Patrick was not even a Roman Catholic. He operated as an independent Christian and a self supporting missionary. And finally, March 17th is not a birthday, but the day the old missionary died in his beloved Ireland.

During his 29 years as a missionary, Patrick baptized over 120,000 Irishmen, and established at least 300 churches.

It's amazing how many fables have become connected with the work of this great missionary. But this is not the first time this has happened.

HIDING JAPANESE SOLDIER

For 26 years after the surrender of Japan in 1945, Japanese soldier Shoichi Yokoi hid in the remote jungles of Guam living on berries, nuts, rats and frogs. Following the creed of soldiers loyal to imperial Japan, he refused to surrender because he did not believe the war was really over. Two local hunters discovered him in January 1972 in a remote jungle. He was wearing a pair of burlap pants and a shirt that he had made from tree bark.

When found, Yokoi was expecting the worst from his American captors. Instead, they gave him a first-class trip back to Japan. His first words to his people were, "It is with much embarrassment that I return." But instead, the Japanese people welcomed him back as a national hero. He became a popular commentator on survival and even ran for parliament!

Many are reluctant and ashamed to surrender to Jesus, believing it is a sign of weakness or that He will rob them of their liberties. In reality, it requires great courage to surrender all to Jesus. And instead of limiting our liberties, Jesus wants to set us free and invites us to reign with Him in heavenly places!

Contents:

MASADA

The term "zealot" in reference to extremists originated from the doomed defenders of Masada, which means "fortress" in Hebrew. This mountaintop stronghold in the Judean desert was built on a rocky mesa rising abruptly 2,000 feet above the nearby Dead Sea.

Herod the Great renovated the fortress between 37 and 31 B.C. When Jerusalem was taken by Rome in A.D. 70, the last remaining rebels, a Jewish sect known as the Zealots, revolted and seized the fortress in their last stand against Roman rule. With plenty of food and water, this group of about a thousand men, women, and children lead by Eleazar ben Jair, held off the Roman army for more than two years!

After the long siege, 15,000 Roman soldiers from the Tenth Legion raised an enormous earth ramp and broke through the walls. They found the bodies of 960 men, women, and children—all victims of a suicide pact to keep the Romans from taking them as slaves. All but seven killed themselves rather than surrender. *But the Bible also teaches that sometimes surrender is the bravest, wisest, and hardest thing to do.*

Luke 8:52 *"And all wept, and bewailed her: but he said, Weep not; she is not dead, but sleepeth."*

PARIS CATACOMBS

One of the more macabre tourist attractions in Paris reopened to the public after a $400,000 facelift. These catacombs of the dead contain the bones of 6 million Parisians.

Curious tourists descend via a narrow spiral staircase into the network of underground passages, where pile upon pile of shin bones lie in neat rows punctuated by a pattern of skulls. The gruesome attraction draws 160,000 visitors a year.

The tunnels were originally stone mines, but later became underground burial chambers when the cemeteries of Paris became so overcrowded and unsanitary in the 18th century, Bones were dug up and stored underground.

Some 190 miles of passageways wind their way under the world's most-visited capital, creating a network of tunnels twice as long as those of the Paris underground metro system. Only one mile of catacombs is open to the public.

An intercom system was added to ensure visitors do not get lost, which should spare anyone else the fate of a hospital worker who decided to explore the tunnels alone during the French Revolution. His skeleton was found 11 years later!

Superstitious visitors are unnerved by the thought that countless spirits of the dead will haunt them for gawking at their disturbed remains. On the other hand, Nestor Valence, who has worked in the subterranean warren for eight years rearranging bones that fall out of place, said he had grown used to the grisly nature of his job. "Touching bones doesn't bother me any more," he says. "When you start, it's a bit weird, but it becomes part of the routine."

So what does the Bible say? Can the dead haunt, spook or curse the living?

AND DID YOU KNOW...

- **Small Hawaii:** The Hawaiian alphabet has 12 letters.
- **Wild World:** Percentage of Africa that is wilderness: 28 percent; Percentage of North America that is wilderness: 38 percent.
- **Mobile Landmarks:** The San Francisco cable cars are the only mobile national monuments.

NAN MADOL

Eight degrees north of the equator in Micronesia, on the remote island of Pohnpei, can be found the haunting ruins of Nan Madol—known also as the Machu Pichu of the Pacific. On this jungle-clad island surrounded by beautiful coral reefs lies a lost city made of bizarre stone "logs."

The ruins of this forgotten civilization is one of archaeology's best-kept secrets and greatest mysteries. Nan Madol, which means "Reef of Heaven", was abandoned centuries ago, yet no other marine city in the world can boast of such a large scale. The ruins cover nearly 150 acres in shallow tidal waters bordering the reef-protected jungle, and a labyrinth of stonewalled canals crisscrosses 92 small man-made islands.

Its major buildings are constructed of giant stone logs that are 18 feet long and several feet in diameter. These logs are made of volcanic basalt crystal and weigh up to two-and-a-half tons. They are stacked like cordwood to form walls up to 50 feet high and 18 feet thick.

The main structures resemble the ceremonial squares constructed by the Mayans and Aztecs. The largest enclosure, approximately one acre in area, contains a central altar that resembles the sacrificial platforms found in Central America. Radiocarbon dating shows Nan Madol was built beginning in the 13th century. More recent discoveries below the tidal level indicate occupation as early as 200 B.C.

It would have required a large organized workforce and sophisticated culture to create this "Venice of the Pacific," but this race of builders has vanished. The reasons for its construction, how the massive stones were transported, or why it was abandoned are all unknown. Even the natives now presently living on Pohnpei are equally mystified by Nan Madol.

CHEOPS PYRAMID

As one of the world's oldest structures (4,600 years), the great Giza pyramid is the sole survivor of the seven wonders of the ancient world. It is believed that a massive, enslaved force of about 25,000 men and women built the colossal structure. It took 20 years to raise, using approximately 2.3 million blocks with an average weight of about 2.5 metric tons. The largest block weighs as much as 15 metric tons.

The pyramid currently stands more than 450 feet high, but at its height it stood 480 feet (50 stories)! It stood as the tallest man-made structure for more than 43 centuries—surpassed only in the nineteenth century. It also boasts a 13.6-acre base.

The sloping angle of its sides is 51 degrees and 51 minutes. Each side is oriented with one of the cardinal points of the compass (north, south, east, west). The pyramid is located at the exact center of the earth's landmass, and the average height of all the land above sea level, as measured only by modern-day technology, is 5,449 inches—the exact height of Cheops.

In addition, the interior stones fit so well that even a business card won't fit between them. It's engineering prowess was so advanced that current technology still can't duplicate the structure.

The pyramid's core was constructed mostly of soft limestone blocks weighing between 4,000 to 40,000 pounds, but the outer layer of the pyramid is crafted in a beautifully bright, protective layer of polished stone superior in durability against the elements. The casing stones, 144,000 in all, were so brilliant that when sunlight reflected off them, they could be seen from the mountains of Israel hundreds of miles away.

These outer "casing stones" are missing today because of a 13th century earthquake, which loosened them. Arabic looters, recognizing this great quarry of precut stones, carted these off to finish construction of palaces and mosques.

The great pyramid represents man's best attempt to build an eternal dwelling on earth but even the pyramids are slowly crumbling. In contrast, Jesus promises to build eternal dwellings for his children where we can abide forever.

John 14:2 "In my Father's house are many mansions: if it were not so, I would have told you. I go to prepare a place for you."

VATICAN CITY

The most populated country in the world is China, with an estimated 1.3 billion citizens. (In fact, the population of China today is greater than the population of the whole world 150 years ago!) But the country with the smallest population is the Vatican.

That's right, in 1929 under the terms of the Lateran Treaty, Vatican City or Holy See was established as an independent state of

109 acres within Rome. Less than a thousand people live in this small country, which is governed by the Pope—who has absolute executive, legislative and judicial powers.

Furthermore, Vatican City has its own currency (equal to the Italian lira) and postal system. It also has a small railroad station and radio station. The city publishes a daily newspaper and monthly journal, and it manages its own telephone and telegraph services. The famous Swiss Guard serves as police, maintaining internal security and protection of the Pope. *Yet despite its tiny territory, Bible prophecy tells that the Vatican will play a major roll in end-time prophecy.*

AND DID YOU KNOW...

- **Flight Nation:** Average number of people airborne over America at any given hour: 61,000.

- **Home Sweet Home:** Half of all Americans live within 50 miles of their birthplace.

- **Ocean Centered:** No matter where you are in Australia, you are never more than 1,000 kilometers from the ocean.

POMPEII

Pompeii: In 80 B.C., Pompeii became a Roman colony; later it was used as a favorite resort for wealthy Romans. It reached a population of about 20,000 at the beginning of the Christian era.

The city was severely damaged by an earthquake in A.D. 63 and then was completely demolished 14 years later by the eruption of the volcano Vesuvius. The blast and resulting carnage completely overwhelmed the towns of Pompeii and Herculaneum. For more than 1,500 years, Pompeii lay undisturbed beneath heaps of ashes and cinders. Not until 1748 were excavations undertaken.

Amazingly, the showers of wet ashes and cinders that accompanied the eruption formed a hermetic seal about the town, preserving many public structures, temples, theaters, baths, shops and private dwellings. In addition, remnants of some of the 2,000 victims of the disaster were found in the ruins, including several gladiators who had been placed in chains to prevent them from escaping or committing suicide.

Ironically, the legion of soldiers most responsible for the sacking of Jerusalem and desecrating the temple were vacationing in Pompeii when it was destroyed.

GOLDEN GATE BRIDGE

When construction began on this incredible feat of engineering on January 5, 1933, Joseph B. Strauss, chief engineer, was adamant about using the most rigorous safety precautions in the history of bridge building. He commissioned a local manufacturer of safety equipment to design protective headgear that Strauss insisted be worn on the job. This prototype of the modern hard hat was worn for the first time along with glare-free goggles. Special hand and face cream protected the workers against the constant biting wind, while special diets helped them fight dizziness. The most conspicuous precaution was the safety net, suspended under the entire floor of the bridge from end to end. During construction, the net saved the lives of 19 men who became known with affection as the *"Half-Way-to-Hell Club."*

Psalm 4:8 "I will both lay me down in peace, and sleep: for thou, LORD, only makest me dwell in safety."

CITY OF REFUGE

On the largest island in Hawaii, ancient ruins of a village stand with a large oblong temple enclosure with walls 1,000 feet long and 700 feet wide. They are also 20 feet thick at the base and rise 20 feet. This temple village was called "Pu 'uhonua"—or the City of Refuge.

When a native Hawaiian committed "Kapu" and broke one of the sacred laws, he was sentenced to death unless he could flee to this village where the "Kahuna Pule" or "big priest" lived. Once inside the walls, he was safe and protected from judgment. Later, the big priest would perform a rite of purification for the guilty party. He could then be declared forgiven, innocent, and was free to begin a new life.

Psalm 33:19-21 "To deliver their soul from death, and to keep them alive in famine. Our soul waiteth for the LORD: he is our help and our shield. For our heart shall rejoice in him, because we have trusted in his holy name."

AND DID YOU KNOW...

- **Longwinded Nationalism:** The Greek national anthem has 158 verses.
- **Higher Leasing:** The University of Texas system is the third-largest landowner in the United States.
- **New Zealand Facts:** The first European to see New Zealand (N.Z.) was Abel Tasman in 1642. The first to set foot on the island was James Cook in 1769. N.Z. was named after Abel Tasman's home district, Zealand, in the Netherlands. Greater Auckland, N.Z. is the second largest city in the world by area, the first being greater Los Angeles. N.Z. has the highest mountain in all of Oceania: Mt. Cook. N.Z. was the first country to give women the vote (1890).

WINCHESTER MANSION

During the height of the Civil War, Sarah Pardee met and married William W. Winchester, the son of the famous rifle manufacturer. They had one child, Annie, who died about one month after birth.

About 15 years later, William died of tuberculosis. The distraught widow was so deeply upset by her losses that she supposedly consulted a spiritualistic medium who explained that the spirits of all those who had been killed by the rifles her family manufactured were seeking revenge by taking the lives of her loved ones. Further, the spirits placed a curse on her that she could only escape by moving west, buying a house and constructing an ever-growing mansion to house good spirits and confound bad ones.

In 1884, Mrs. Winchester moved to San Jose, California, and purchased an eight-room farmhouse. She then began her never-ending building project. With a great deal of money and few responsibilities, she kept a staff of up to 60 servants and carpenters constantly busy. She had no master plan and according to her carpenters, she built whenever, wherever and however she pleased—as directed by the spirits.

Each night, Sarah visited a séance room to receive messages from the spirits telling her what she should build. These bizarre orders resulted in many strange creations, such as doors that open to walls, stairs that head into ceilings, and a cupboard with only half-an-inch of storage space. The rambling structure has 160 rooms, 2,000 doors, 10,0000 windows, and 150,000 panes of glass. It also boasts 40 stairways, 47 fireplaces, and 13 bathrooms.

Sarah paid her workers well to keep building continuously for nearly 40 years, until she died in 1922. One carpenter worked for her for 36 years. Sarah Winchester was a very lonely woman, and there is only one blurry photograph of this eccentric recluse. In fact, when President Theodore Roosevelt came to visit San Jose, the Chamber of Commerce tried to get Mrs. Winchester to receive him, but she refused.

All this wasted money, labor and years of fear to appease the supposed spirits of the dead is astounding. But can the spirits of the dead really haunt the living?

THE WORLD TRADE CENTER

Until the events of September 11, 2001, the tallest building in New York City, and the second tallest in the world, was the World Trade Center. More than 30 million people had visited the observation deck at the top. Each day, more than 250,000 people worked in or visited the World Trade Center—that's nearly half of the people that live in Wyoming!

During its construction, 1.2 million cubic yards of earth were excavated and placed in the Hudson River, which created more than 23 acres of new land for Battery Park. The 425,000 cubic yards of concrete used in building the World Trade Center was enough to build a five-foot wide sidewalk from New York City to Washington D.C.

The center was the largest "office building" in the world, with 12 million square feet of rental space. Each twin tower had 99 elevators, but the two express elevators traveled 107 floors in less than a minute—that's faster than 25 feet per second! The 43,600 windows were cleaned by automatic window washing machines.

On May 26, 1977, George Willig suction-cupped his way up the northeast wall to the "Top of the World" look out! On August 7, 1974, Philippe Petit tight-roped between the twin structures. And several adventurers have parachuted from the top. The two towers of the World Trade Center dominated New York's vista and were the first thing you noticed when approaching on a clear day.

Christ's return will far exceed these giants dominance of the sky. In Matthew 24:27, we're told that "For as the lightning cometh out of the east, and shineth even unto the west; so shall also the coming of the Son of man be."

THE UNIVERSE

Looking up at the clear, night sky, you can see about as much of the universe as a single-cell amoeba might see of the ocean in which it swims. The moon, the planets and the few thousand stars that are visible to us are merely a single drop of water in the boundless sea of the universe.

The distance from our galaxy to the next nearest one is almost one-and-a-half million light-years. And the known universe is believed to be about 10 to 12 billion light years long.

The disc-shaped galaxy to which our sun belongs is called the Milky Way, which is a family of more than 100 billion stars. Astronomers say there are as many as 100 billion other galaxies in the universe, many much bigger than our own. Statistical probability dictates that among these trillions of stars, there may be millions of inhabitable planets.

Yet the scriptures tell us that someday, the God who spoke these things into existence will move the capitol of the whole universe to our puny planet.

THE DEAD SEA

At 1,312 feet below sea level in Israel, the Dead Sea is one of the lowest water surfaces on earth—and one of the most unusual spots on the planet.

The sea receives more than 6 million tons of water every day from the Jordan River alone, but even though it has no outlet, the water level never rises!

Geographers used to believe there was an enormous chasm in the bottom of the Dead Sea in which its water poured down into the earth. But U.S. Navy sound tests disproved that theory.

The real answer lies in the fact that the seabed is 47 miles long and an average of 9 miles wide; therefore, evaporation in that seething desert basin exceeds the watery input, also making the sea seven times as salty as the ocean.

Because of its high mineral content, no one can sink or drown while bathing there. It is said that Vespasian, an ancient Roman commander, heard this fact and tested it by ordering bound slaves to be thrown in. The slaves floated.

This high concentration of minerals also makes the Dead Sea one of the most valuable spots on earth. Among its precious minerals is potash, which is often used in explosives and fertilizer. It has been estimated that the Dead Sea has enough potash to provide the entire world's fertilizer needs for 2,000 years.

It also has an estimated 22 billion tons of magnesium chloride, 12 billion tons of common salt, 6 billion tons of calcium chloride, 2 billion tons of potassium chloride, 1 billion tons of magnesium bromide. The value of these chemicals comes to a staggering $1,270,000,000,000. All the goods exported from Israel are nothing compared to the enormous mineral wealth in the Dead Sea.

Who would dream that a place that is so outwardly lifeless could be so valuable? Perhaps you have also underestimated your worth before God?

Matthew 10:28-31 "And fear not them which kill the body, but are not able to kill the soul: but rather fear him which is able to destroy both soul and body in hell. Are not two sparrows sold for a farthing? and one of them shall not fall on the ground without your Father. But the very hairs of your head are all numbered. Fear ye not therefore, ye are of more value than many sparrows."

BIOSPHERE 2

This state-of-the-art greenhouse built on three-acres in the Arizona desert is a giant, computer controlled environment. It was intended to be a miniature version of the much larger biosphere 1, better known as earth. Completed in 1991 at a cost of $200 million, it includes five wilderness areas, ranging from a rain forest to a desert, and is stocked with thousands of exotic plants and animals. Eight humans ("biospherians") were to learn how to live off the land, isolated from the outside world except for communications. The designers envisioned Biosphere 2 as the first step toward human colonization of Mars.

But when this landlocked Noah's Ark set sail for a two-year voyage of discovery from 1991–93, it ran aground on a host of unforeseen environmental and human disasters. Oxygen levels inside the complex dropped so low that emergency oxygen was pumped in—violating the main tenet of isolation. And crop production was so poor that the starving crew got hungry enough to steal food from one another or have it smuggled in. Nearly all the birds and animals that were supposed to thrive inside died—except for "crazy ants" and cockroaches that now fill the place.

Their proud vision of man making utopia on earth became a joke—today Biosphere 2 is a tourist attraction masquerading as science.

Matthew 6:20 "But lay up for yourselves treasures in heaven, where neither moth nor rust doth corrupt, and where thieves do not break through nor steal: ... "

AND DID YOU KNOW...

- **National Parks:** Yellowstone was the first national park (1872) but the first area to be set aside under federal protection was Hot Springs Reservation, Arkansas (1832). It became Hot Springs National Park in 1921.

- **Gateway:** The official name of the St. Louis Gateway Arch is "The Jefferson National Expansion Monument." The Gateway Arch looks taller than it is wider, but it is exactly 630 feet by 630 feet.

- **Close, but no...** Everybody knows that St. Augustine, Florida, is the oldest city in the nation, but not everybody knows that St. Mary's, Georgia is the second oldest.

TAJ MAHAL

Located in Agra, India, the Taj Mahal is considered one of the seven wonders of the modern world. Beginning in 1631, the perfectly symmetrical building, a tomb for the wife of a 17th-century emperor, was constructed over a span of 17 years by 20,000 workers. This beautiful massive-domed structure was designed in the Indo-Islamic style using white marble and inlaid gems. Each corner has a prayer tower, and passages from the Koran adorn the outside walls. The bodies of the emperor and his wife remain in a vault below the building.

In the 1830s, the British scheduled to demolish the Taj Mahal and auction off the marble in London. Demolition machines were brought into the gardens and were about to begin work, when word came from London that the price of white marble was so low it would not be worth the trouble to tear it down.

AND DID YOU KNOW...

- **Presidential Vacations:** The presidential retreat in Maryland was originally called "Shangri-La." It was renamed "Camp David" by President Eisenhower in 1953 for his grandson.

- **Ancient Facts:** If you took all the stone from the three Egyptian pyramids at Giza, you could build a wall one foot wide, and ten feet tall around France.

- **Endangered Planet:** Rainforests cover less than two percent of the earth's surface, yet they are home to some 50 to 70 percent of all life forms on our planet.

- **Denver Firsts:** The first license plate on a car in the United States was issued in Denver, Colorado in 1908.

THE TEMPLE OF SOLOMON

One of the seven wonders of the ancient world was the Temple of Solomon that was demolished by King Nebuchadnezzar and the materials were taken back to Babylon. Many believe that the Jewish temple will be rebuilt before the Anti-Christ seizes power and Jesus returns.

AND DID YOU KNOW...

- **Soho:** According to the London for Visitors Web site, the area known as Soho used to be part of King Henry VIII's hunting grounds. When a hunter spied a deer, he yelled "Tally-Ho!," but when he found a smaller prey, the cry became "So-Ho!" As the area was developed, the name stuck.

- **You Always Need Cash:** There is an ATM at McMurdo Station in Antarctica, which has a winter population of 200.

- **Century Russians:** There are more 100 dollar bills in Russia currently than there are in the United States.

- **Say that Again?** South Africa used to have two official languages. Now it has 11.

THE EMPIRE STATE BUILDING

This architectural achievement completed in 1931 was known for many years as the tallest building in the world—standing at 1250 ft. and boasting 102 stories of office space. It no longer holds that distinction, having been surpassed in height by several taller structures both in the United States and in Asia. But because it was built of prefabricated blocks, it was completed in less than two years, and the construction records that it set in the process have never been broken. In fact, one 14-floor section was erected in less than a week.

THE CATACOMBS

The Christians of the ancient Mediterranean world used this network of subterranean chambers and galleries for burial. But during times of persecution, the catacombs became places of refuge because burial grounds were sacrosanct by Roman law. When churches above ground were destroyed by imperial order, worshippers met in the catacomb chapels. By the A.D. 200, Christians had carved 600 miles of tombs in volcanic rock around Rome.

As Christianity gained converts and burials multiplied, the catacombs were expanded into honeycombs of galleries. When one level was no longer sufficient, staircases were dug and a second, third, and even fourth level of galleries was excavated. Archeologists estimate that approximately 3 million Christians were interned in the catacombs around Rome. Romans preferred cremation, but the Christians followed the practice of interring the dead in catacombs, which they called *koimeteria,* or "sleeping places," to suggest that, for a Christian, death is merely sleep before resurrection.

AND DID YOU KNOW...

- **Slow Day:** On March 29, 1848, Niagara Falls stopped flowing for 30 hours because of an ice jam blocking the Niagara River.

- **Dead-fast Rules:** In Italy, it is illegal to make coffins out of anything except nutshells or wood.

- **Cuckoo Misconception:** Contrary to popular folklore, cuckoo clocks do not come from Switzerland but from the Black Forest in Germany.

- **U.S. Army Park Service?** The first national park, Yellowstone, was proclaimed a national park in 1872. However, there was no National Park Service until 1916. Until then, the U.S. Army administered the parks. When the Park Service was formed, they got their first uniforms from the Army, hence the ranger (campaign) hats.

THE SARGASSO SEA

One of the most interesting places in the world is in the middle of the Atlantic. The Sargasso Sea does not have a coastline, but rather is a separate sea located between the West Indies and the Azores. Its warm waters cover some 2 million square miles and are encircled by the Gulf Stream causing the oval-shaped sea to move in a slow, clockwise drift. This makes the three-mile deep waters exceptionally clear and blue, with a high salt content.

The Sargasso Sea is filled with seaweed. Early Portuguese navigators named the sea "sargaco," the word for grape, after the bulbous little floats on the Sargassum seaweed. Although one-third of the Atlantic's plankton is produced there, the sea is known as "the floating desert" because its seaweed lacks the nutrients to attract commercially valuable fish. But many small marine animals, including tiny crabs, shrimp, and octopuses, live on and among the sea-weed. One of the most amazing facts about the Sargasso Sea is that it serves as the international meeting place for eels. Drawn by unknown forces, each fall millions of these snakelike fish migrate from Europe, the Mediterranean, and the United States to mate, spawn, and die. Some eels have even left their fresh water homes and crossed miles of land, breathing through their skin, to reach the sea to breed. Once the eggs hatch, their inch-long, transparent larvae known as "glass eels" make the long journey back to continental streams and rivers. This journey can take up to three years, during which many of them will be eaten by a multitude of oceanic predators.

For hundreds of years, naturalists wondered where eels came from. When it was discovered that virtually all the eels in the Western Hemisphere come from the Sargasso Sea, it came as an amazing revelation.

AND DID YOU KNOW...

- **Small Capital:** With a population of fewer than 9,000, Montpelier, Vermont is the smallest state capital in the nation.

- **Who's Bigger:** Due to precipitation, for a few weeks, K2 is taller than Mt. Everest

- **Hot Days:** The highest temperature ever recorded on Earth was 136 degrees Fahrenheit on September 13, 1992, in Azizia, Libya.

PANAMA CANAL

The canal across the Isthmus of Panama in Central America is one of the greatest engineering marvels of the past 1,000 years. In 1513, Vasco de Balboa's discovery of the Pacific coast of Panama soon had merchants and empire-builders dreaming of a shortcut that would enable ships to sail westward from the Atlantic to the Pacific without making the grueling, 12,000-mile journey around the tip of South America. Over the next 200 years, visionaries ranging from Benjamin Franklin to Simon Bolivar advocated the digging of a channel. Several countries and companies either quit or went bankrupt attempting to build the canal, but it was finally completed by the United States under Teddy Roosevelt from 1904 to 1914. At that time, it was the largest and most complex project of its kind ever undertaken, employing tens of thousands of workers and costing $350 million.

The 50-mile canal handles a large volume of the world's shipping, enabling vessels to travel between the Pacific and Atlantic oceans without traveling around South America, reducing their voyages by thousands of miles and dollars.

The canal consists of artificially created lakes, channels, and a series of locks, or water-filled chambers, that raise and lower ships 85 feet through the mountainous terrain of central Panama. Battleships and destroyers of the world are built to squeeze through the small 80-year old locks. The canal's 12 locks (3 sets of double locks at each end) have the same dimensions: 110-feet wide by 1,000-feet long with gates at each end. Water enters and leaves each lock through a system of large culverts or tunnels that were built by the same man who built New York's subways. About 52 million gallons of gravity-flow water are used to transfer each ship through the canal. Because the "S" shape of the Isthmus of Panama, a ship sailing through the canal will actually travel west to east to go east to west.

The canal commission recruited more than 50,000 laborers, mostly from nearby Caribbean islands, to work on the canal. In all, another 100,000 people migrated to Panama during the construction era, adding to the diversity of Panama's population. The Panama Canal was also the costliest modern project in terms of lives lost. In the 40 years, various countries worked on the canal, more than 30,000 people died. Amazingly, it was not the mountains that killed most of the workers but the mosquitoes! Finally William C. Gorgas staged a successful campaign to eradicate the mosquitoes and yellow fever disappeared. Likewise today, the number one killer in North America is not from using firearms but eating with dinner forks!

HADRIAN'S WALL

Around A.D. 122, Roman Emperor Hadrian ordered the construction of a wall in northern Britain, then part of the Roman Empire, to keep out the unconquered Caledonians of Scotland. Built out of stone and turf and measuring about 73 miles in length, the wall linked a series of forts and watchtowers. It stood about 20 feet high. The Romans rebuilt Hadrian's Wall several times throughout the third and fourth centuries and used it as a fortification until about 400. A military road ran along the south side of the wall, and a series of heavily garrisoned forts and sentry posts were built along its length. The wall also marked the frontier of Roman civil jurisdiction. A few sections of Hadrian's Wall remain standing in present-day Great Britain.

Psalm 122:7 "*Peace be within thy walls, and prosperity within thy palaces.*"

CHATEAU PERFUMES

The Chateau near Paris, long inhabited by first wife of Napoleon, Empress Josephine, still exudes the strong odor of musk with which the empress used to douse her person. The castle, now a museum, changed hands many times after Napoleon's wife died in it in 1814. But no effort of the subsequent owners has ever succeeded in eradicating the strong and penetrating scent that clings to the walls, imprinting the empress' personality on her residence forever. Napoleon was so enamored of the sweet smell of success that he used 54 bottles of cologne a month and carried them with him to his battlefields. One would think that on a windy day the odor would have alerted the enemy of his presence.

ANCIENT BABYLON

Ancient Babylon reached its greatest glory during the reign of King Nebuchadnezzar (604–562 B.C.) and was probably the largest city of antiquity. Babylon was an immense square, totaling 15 miles on each side with Marduk's Temple and the Tower of Babylon at its center. It was divided into two equal parts by the Euphrates running under the walls, which also served to irrigate and air condition the entire metropolis.

Babylon had 25 avenues, 150 feet wide, which ran across the city from north to south. The same number crossed them at right angles from east to west, making a total of 676 great blocks, each nearly 3/4 square miles. Nebuchadnezzar also built massive fortifications with thick walls that measured from 67 feet at the base to 54 feet at the top—four chariots could race abreast on the top of the walls.

Not only was ancient Babylon big, it was beautiful! The public buildings were faced with bright glazed bricks in different colors. The outer walls of the city were yellow, the gates blue, the palaces rose-red, and the temples white. All this, plus the famous hanging gardens, gave this metropolis a splendor that was unequaled by any other earthly city.

Yet God prophesied that ancient Babylon would be destroyed and never be rebuilt.

WATERLOO BIRD NEST

A prominent hill featuring a colossal statue of a great lion perched on a tall stone pedestal commemorates the historic battle of Waterloo. It's menacing, open-mouthed figure snarls a warning to would-be despots. The story is that the lion was forged from the many cannons left strewn across the famous battlefield. Once, a tiny bird tended her young within the gaping jaws of the lion—a strange picture: the little birds snugly living between the teeth of a huge lion. *It reminds us that when believers fully trust their lives in the* LORD's *keeping, we'll have peace that passes all understanding. "He who dwells in the secret place of the Most High shall abide under the shadow of the Almighty." (Psalm 91:1).*

AND DID YOU KNOW...

- **A Snow Day:** The record for most snowfall in a day, 78 inches, was made on February 7, 1916, in Alaska.

- **Where's that Shirt?** During the California Gold Rush, Boston ships carried the laundry of the gold miners all the way across the Pacific to Canton, China, to be laundered and starched. It took a year before the miner received his laundry back.

- **Geyser Central:** There are more geysers in Yellowstone National Park than there are in the entire rest of the world.

- **Tallest Mountain:** Technically, Mt. Everest is not the tallest mountain. Mauna Kea Mountain on the Island of Hawaii is 230 meters taller—4,201m above water and 4,877 underwater! Everest is only 8,848m.

FASCINATING SCIENCE

Contents:

EFFECTIVE PLACEBO

A placebo is a harmless pill or solution made from a neutral substance, such as sugar or starch, that is used to avoid bias when testing new drugs. But in some tests, patients have experienced dramatic results from these placebos based simply on their belief that the pill will help them.

Doctors have administered placebos to patients who are thought to have incurable illnesses to induce the so-called placebo effect: a temporary, or even permanent, improvement of the patient's condition—which might correspond to their faith in the doctor or medicine. In 1955, a study by Dr. Henry Knowles Beecher reports that 35 percent of patients had their conditions improved by receiving placebos.

Little is understood of how this works, but one theory is that the patient's faith in a cure might be related to the release of brain chemicals that help promote healing. Perhaps this is why Jesus always said to those he healed, "Your faith has made you whole."

Modern medicine is returning to the conclusion that a person's faith has a great deal to do with their rate of recovery. In fact, the May 2001, Reader's Digest reports a nationwide study found those who attend religious services more than once a week have a seven-year longer life expectancy than those who never attend. The Bible also teaches that a person's eternal life expectancy is directly connected with their faith.

STAR STUFF

About 5,000 stars can be seen with the naked eye, but a small telescope can reveal hundreds of thousands! The largest telescopes on earth disclose millions of galaxies packed with stars, where as the Hubble telescope in space may be able to see over a billion galaxies, which are ensembles of stars, gravitationally interacting and orbiting around a common center. The Andromeda Galaxy is the object farthest from earth still visible with the naked eye. It can be seen from the Northern Hemisphere in the constellation Andromeda.

Now imagine this: Each galaxy is estimated to contain more than 200 billion stars. It's estimated that 125 billion galaxies exist in the universe. It's believed there are more than 1x1022 stars in the universe (1 followed by 22 zeros)!

All the stars visible to the unaided eye are in the Milky Way. The sun is just one star in this galaxy. The Milky Way is a spiral galaxy with a diameter of 100,000 light-years across. That means that traveling at the speed of light (approximately 186,000 mile per second), it will take 100,000 years to span the diameter.

The central "bulge" of this spiral is about 10,000 light-years thick. The center is in the direction of Sagittarius and is about 23,000 light-years from our sun. The largest stars of the Milky Way would easily consume our planet, Mars, Jupiter and Saturn if placed where the sun is now.

The smallest white dwarf stars are about the size of earth, and neutron stars can be less than 10 miles in diameter. The nearest star, Alpha Centauri, is about 4.3 light years away. Stars are made chiefly of hot, glowing hydrogen and a smaller amount of helium. The outer layers of some stars are so empty that they can be described as red-hot vacuums. Other stars are so dense that a teaspoonful of the material would weigh several tons.

Such awesome facts stir within us a yearning for space travel. But did you know that the Bible teaches that the redeemed will have this opportunity?

LIGHTNING LORE

This visible, electric discharge between rain clouds or between a rain cloud and the earth is seen in the form of a brilliant arc—sometimes several miles long. The discharge creates a sound wave that is heard as thunder. Some strokes may even move from ground to cloud, particularly from mountain peaks and from tall objects such as radio towers. Lightning flashes from a cloud to the earth may be less than 3,000 feet in length, while flashes from one cloud to another have been recorded more than 20 miles long. Only one lightning flash in a hundred ever strikes the earth.

However, contrary to the belief that lightning never strikes the same spot twice, it has been known to strike one object or person many times during an intense electrical storm. During one storm, the Empire State Building was struck 15 times within 15 minutes. Sometimes a stroke of lightning consists of as many as 42 discharges that strike the same spot in such quick succession that they appear to be a single flash. It all happens in less than a fourth of a second!

Lightning is one of nature's most violent acts. Each year, it destroys hundreds of millions of dollars of property, mostly from forest and home fires. Lightning also causes well over 100 fatalities each year, which adds up to more casualties than from any other natural disaster. Brescia, Italy, is a place where one of the worst lightning tragedies occurred. In 1769, a flash hit the state arsenal, exploding more than 100 tons of gunpowder and killing 3,000 people.

Animals seem to be more susceptible to death by lightning than humans. In many cases, a flash has killed only one man in a crowd, while other flashes have killed all the animals in a large group. As examples, 340 sheep were killed in France in 1890 from a single flash in an open field.

The rarest and least understood form of lightning is "ball lightning," a slow-moving globe of fire that varies in diameter, usually between two and 20 inches. Occurring during heavy thunderstorms, it is usually seen traveling horizontally a few feet from the ground. One of the most remarkable examples appeared in Milan. It floated so slowly down the middle of a street that a crowd of boys were able to walk beside it for half a mile before it struck an obstacle and exploded harmlessly.

More electricity is produced from lightning strikes each day than all the man-made generators can produce in a year, but science has never found a practical way to harness this power.

*In **Matthew 24:27**, Jesus says, "For as the lightning comes from the* *east and flashes to the west, so also will the coming of the Son of Man be." (NKJV) Yet in spite of this some still believe his return will be a secret.*

DREARY DOLDRUMS

Nothing was so feared by seamen in the days when ocean vessels were driven by wind and sail than the doldrums. The doldrums is a part of the ocean near the equator, abounding with prolonged calms and light, baffling winds. The old sailing vessels, when caught in doldrums, would sometimes lie helpless for days and weeks, waiting for the wind to begin to blow. There the weather is hot, humid, and extremely dispiriting—sometimes it drove the irritable sailors to violence or insanity. Surprisingly, most hurricanes and severe squalls also originate within the doldrums.

Psalm 107:25 "For he commandeth, and raiseth the stormy wind, which lifteth up the waves thereof."

BLACK HOLES

By 1999, astronomers had found only a dozen potential black holes in our observable universe. This unique phenomenon in space is caused by objects with such concentrated mass that their immense gravitational pull even sucks in light. A star with ten times the mass of our sun would become a black hole if it were compressed to 60 miles or less in diameter.

The minimum speed required to escape earth's gravitational pull is called the "escape velocity." Now imagine an object with a required escape velocity greater than the velocity of light (186,000 mile per second)! Since nothing as yet discovered can travel faster than light, nothing could escape the object's gravitational pull!

The gravitational force of black holes is so strong that laws of physics no longer apply. Astronomers must use Einstein's theory of relativity to explain the behavior of light and matter under such strong forces. You might be wondering, what causes matter to become so concentrated as to produce a black hole? It occurs when a star dies and the core continues to collapse, forming a super dense mass that nothing can escape.

The Bible teaches us that when Lucifer fell, he imploded like a fallen star and refuses to allow the light of truth to escape his domain.

MAGNETITE

Those electronic metal detectors stationed at airports and government buildings that check for concealed weapons are not exactly new. Centuries ago, one of the royal palaces in Chang-an, the ancient Chinese capital now known as Sian, had gates made of lodestone. Lodestone is a powerful natural magnet also known as magnetite, which is a crystallized iron mineral with a black metallic luster.

If a would-be assassin came through these palace gates with a concealed dagger, the lodestone would pull at the hidden iron weapon like an invisible hand. The startled criminal would instinctively reach for the weapon. Trained guards stationed by the magic gate carefully watched for every movement, and would then spring forward and search the suspect.

Because the superstitious people believed the ruler had special powers to read their hearts, few ever entertained thoughts of assassination. *The Bible promises in Isaiah 54:17 that no weapon formed against God's people prosper.*

Isaiah 54:17 "No weapon that is formed against thee shall prosper; and every tongue that shall rise against thee in judgment thou shalt condemn. This is the heritage of the servants of the LORD, and their righteousness is of me, saith the LORD."

AND DID YOU KNOW...

- **Slow Fall:** When Heinz Ketchup leaves the bottle, it travels at a rate of 25 miles per year.

- **Kiloton Storms:** In 10 minutes, a hurricane releases more energy than all the world's nuclear weapons combined.

- **Strange Math:** 111,111,111 x 111,111,111 equals 12,345,678,987,654,321

SEARING SUN

Our fantastically hot cosmic radiation powerhouse has a surface temperature of about 11,000 degrees, and its interior temperature is estimated as high as 18 million degrees. The sun is so colossal in size that it contains 99.8 percent of the total mass of our solar system. It would take more than a million earths to fill its core. Because it's some 93 million miles away, it takes the light from the sun about eight minutes and 20 seconds to reach us.

The pressure at the center of the sun is about 700 million tons per square inch. It's enough to smash atoms, expose the inner nuclei, and allow them to smash into each other, interact, and produce the radiation that gives off light and warmth. In fact, the material at the core of the sun is so hot that if you could capture enough to cover a pinhead, it would radiate enough heat to kill a man 1 mile away.

So you can understand why many of the ancient pagan civilizations worshiped the sun, but how much better it would be if they had worshiped the one who made the sun!

AND DID YOU KNOW...

- **First Words:** The first phone message, spoken by Alexander Graham Bell on March 10, 1876, to his assistant Thomas Augustus Watson, was "Mr. Watson, come here I need you."

- **Forward Forty:** Forty is the only number spelled sequentially!

- **Vintage Calorie:** It takes a week to make a jellybean.

- **Lots of Sneezes:** One ragweed plant can release as many as one billion grains of pollen.

- **The Worst Dentist:** The electric chair was invented by a dentist.

JUMPIN' JUPITER

This king of planets is two-and-a-half times larger than all the other planets, satellites, asteroids and comets of our solar system combined. Yet, despite its immense size, Jupiter has the shortest day! With a circumference of 280,000 miles (ours is merely 25,000), Jupiter still manages to make one turn every nine hours and fifty-five minutes! Jupiter's Great Red Spot is 25,000 miles wide. It is thought be the vortex of a hurricane that has been whirling for at least seven centuries.

In Roman mythology Jupiter or Jove was the ruler of the gods. Originally the god of the sky and king of heaven, Jupiter was later worshiped as god of rain, thunder, and lightning. As the protector of Rome, he was called Jupiter Optimus Maximus ("the best and greatest").

What was it that led the great civilizations like Rome and Greece to worship the creation instead of the creator?

PHOTOSYNTHESIS

This is the process by which chlorophyll-containing organisms, such as green plants, algae, and some bacteria, capture energy in the form of light and convert it to chemical energy while also transforming carbon dioxide into life-giving oxygen. Virtually all the energy available for life on earth is made available through photosynthesis.

To produce the same amount of energy that trees and plants produce from sunlight in one day would require all the coal in 20,500,000 coal cars or the equivalent of a coal train that wraps around the world six times!

It takes almost nine minutes for a photon of light to travel the 93 million miles from the sun to the earth, but a plant needs only a few trillionths of a second to capture the light energy, process it, and store it in the form of a chemical bond!

The bread we eat, the air we breathe, and even the wood we use to build our homes comes through this miraculous process— lasagna, lumber and air for our lungs come from sunlight.

NASA scientists have studied this process for years, knowing that it is the secret to long-term space travel. However, so far man has been unable to duplicate what God does so easily through plants!

Matthew 5:16 "Let your light so shine before men, that they may see your good works, and glorify your Father which is in heaven."

WORD WONDERS

Scientists say that sound waves set in motion by our voices go on an endless journey through space. If we had the power to stand on some distant planet long years afterwards, with instruments delicate enough, we might be able to find those sounds again and recreate the words we spoke here on earth.

Repeated studies show that the ear is superior to the eye and people remember more from words they hear than words they see. In fact, the mind is able to understand a spoken word in 140 milliseconds, while it takes 180 milliseconds to understand the printed word! Why? Psychologists believe this 40-millisecond delay occurs while the brain translates the visual data into aural sounds it can understand.

Psalm 119:129-130 "Thy testimonies are wonderful: therefore doth my soul keep them. The entrance of thy words giveth light; it giveth understanding unto the simple."

AND DID YOU KNOW...

- **Great Big Light:** The sun is 330,330 times larger than the earth.

- **False Advertising:** A ten-gallon hat holds less than a gallon.

- **Nightlight:** Thomas Edison, light bulb inventor, was afraid of the dark!

- **Light Shows:** Lightning strikes the earth 100 times every second of the day.

- **Solar System Rebel:** Venus is the only planet that rotates clockwise.

GOOD AS GOLD

Gold is the most malleable and ductile of all the metals. It can easily be beaten or hammered to a thickness of 0.000005 inches. Just one ounce of gold can be drawn into a wire more than 50 miles long.

This precious metal occurs in seawater to the extent of up to 250 parts by weight to 100 million parts of water. Although the quantity of gold present in seawater is more than 9 billion metric tons, the cost of recovering the gold would be far greater than the value of the gold.

In 1848, the western gold fields were found in California during excavation for a sawmill east of Sacramento. During the next five years, $285 million dollars of gold was procured—nearly 21 times greater than the total previous production of the entire country.

Coinage gold is composed of 90 parts gold to 10 parts silver. Green gold used in jewelry contains copper and silver; white gold contains zinc and nickel or platinum metals. Radioisotopes of gold are used in biological research and in the treatment of cancer. Gold is also used in treating arthritis.

Gold appears in the Bible more than 450 times—perhaps most awe-inspiring in *Revelation 21:18*. The construction of the walls of New Jerusalem is of jasper; and the city is of pure gold—like clear glass. This is where the saved will live after the return of Jesus.

AND DID YOU KNOW...

- **Bow Facts:** A rainbow can only be seen in the morning or late afternoon and can only occur when the sun is 40 degrees or less above the horizon.

- **Naming Boulders:** A large amount of boulders that have fallen off a cliff is known as *talus*, whereas they would be known as *moraine* had they been left there by a glacier.

- **Sick Efficiency:** A typical American hospital has three to four times more employees than patients.

- **Fearful Words:** *Taphephobia* is the fear of being buried alive; *Clinophobia* is the fear of beds; *Triskaidekaphobia* is the fear of the number "13".

- **Stormy World:** At any given time there are at least 1,800 thunderstorms around the world.

FOOL'S GOLD

Gold coinage is composed of 90 parts gold to 10 parts silver. But counterfeit gold, or "fools gold," is made of iron pyrites, which is a mineral composed of iron sulfide, the most common sulfide mineral. The mineral is brass yellow, or opaque, and has a metallic luster. The resemblance of pyrite to gold caused many prospectors to mistake it for gold. Even though it is often associated with gold or copper it is easily distinguished by its unusual brittleness.

This dynamic is also seen in the area of spiritual truth. Millions of people are toting around heavy bags bulging with fool's gold. They rejoice that they have discovered that which will make them rich, but though it sparkles on the outside it will be discovered useless at the bank of heaven.

Matthew 6:19-21 "Lay not up for yourselves treasures upon earth,

*where moth and rust doth corrupt, and where thieves break through and
steal: But lay up for yourselves treasures in heaven, where neither moth
nor rust doth corrupt, and where thieves do not break through nor steal:
For where your treasure is, there will your heart be also."*

THE EARTH'S CIRCUMFERENCE

At the equator, the earth's perimeter is 24,902 miles long. The
Italian-born navigator Christopher Columbus correctly believed
that one could reach the east by sailing west, but he underestimated
the size of the planet. Therefore, when he reached the Caribbean, he
thought he was in India and called the natives "Indians." The earth
is actually more than three times bigger than Columbus first
thought! It's good that he took some extra food along the way!

SLEEP DEPRIVATION

Did you know that just one hour of sleep deprivation increases
the number of highway accidents by eight percent, and an hour of
extra sleep decreases them by 8 percent? It's true! And it happens
every year during the daylight savings time changes.

Your driving capability after you have been awake for 18 hours
is the same as driving after you have had two alcoholic drinks. When
you have been awake for 24 hours, you're driving no differently than
if you've had six drinks! Optimum performance comes with nine
hours of sleep each night.

*Getting enough sleep is important when it comes to performance,
but Jesus said there is a time to stay awake at any cost.*

HOLY HAILSTONES

The heaviest U.S. hailstone on record fell in Coffeyville, Kansas,
on September 3, 1970. It weighed 1.6 pounds and had a circumference of 17.5 inches and a diameter of 5.62 inches. The world-record
holding hailstone weighed 2.25 pounds and fell in Bangladesh in
1986. It reportedly killed 92 people!

*This is impressive, but the Bible predicts that the mother of all hail-
storms is still in the future.*

SATELLITES

Since the launching of Sputnik 1, the first artificial satellite in 1957, thousands of "man-made moons" have been fired into earth's orbit. The first living creature launched into space was Laika, a dog. On November 3, 1957, the Soviets flew Laika inside a pressurized chamber aboard the satellite Sputnik 2.

Television uses satellites locked in a geo-stationary orbit. They circle the earth around the equator at a very specific altitude that allows them to complete one orbit in the same amount of time that it takes the earth to rotate once. As a result, these satellites stay 22,200 miles above one fixed point on the earth's equator at all times.

Today, artificial satellites play a key role in military intelligence, the study of earth and space, and in communications. The Lord is using these man-made planets to ricochet the gospel to every major continent!

THE BLACK DEATH

This particularly nasty form of bubonic plague has killed tens of millions of people since it first appeared in the 14th-century. It is caused by the bacterium carried by infected fleas and rats. In most cases, the infected victim suffers from fever, chills, fatigue, and painfully swollen lymph nodes. The 14th-century plague acquired its name from another symptom: hemorrhages that turned black.

The Black Death is traced to the Gobi Desert in the 1320s. By 1400, it invaded China and reduced its population from 125 million to 90 million. It then followed trade routes west to India, the Middle East, and finally into Europe. In Cairo, Egypt, a city of 500,000, at the height of the epidemic, 7,000 people died each day. By 1349, the plague had killed one-third of the population of the Muslim world.

In 1347, the Eurasian nomads deliberately infected a European community with the disease. While laying siege to a Genoese trading post in the Crimea, they lobbed plague-infected corpses into the town by catapult. From the Crimea, the Genoese inadvertently brought the disease to Sicily in a ship carrying infected rats. It swept through Sicily in 1347; North Africa, Italy, France, and Spain in 1348; Hungary, Austria, Switzerland, England, Germany, and the Low Countries in 1349; and reached Scandinavia in 1350. Norsemen carried the disease to faraway Iceland and probably to Greenland, where the plague has-tened the end of the Viking settlements. Some 25 million Europeans were killed by the initial onslaught of the Black Death; whole villages were wiped out.

In its course, the Black Death carried away a greater proportion of the world's people than any other disease or war in history. It literally transformed European society—reducing the population by one-third.

At its peak, no medical shield could protect against the Black Death, but today we know that a vaccine can be produced from a transfusion of somebody who was exposed to the plague without being overcome by it. *Likewise, our only cure for sin is to receive a blood transfusion from Jesus, the only one who was exposed to sin without being overcome by it.*

AMAZING WATER

- 75 percent of Americans are chronically dehydrated.
- In 37 percent, the thirst mechanism is so weak that it is often mistaken for hunger.
- Mild dehydration will slow down metabolism as much as 3 percent.
- Lack of water is the number-one trigger of daytime fatigue.
- One study revealed that one glass of water shuts down midnight hunger pangs for nearly every dieter studied.
- Some research indicates that 8 to 10 glasses of water a day could significantly ease back and joint pain.
- A mere two percent drop in body water can trigger fuzzy short-term memory, trouble with basic math, and difficulty focusing on the computer screen or on a printed page.
- Drinking five glasses of water daily decreases the risk of colon cancer by 45 percent, plus it can slash the risk of breast cancer by 79 percent and bladder cancer by 50 percent.

It's obvious that sufficient water can eliminate or ease a whole host of common health problems. *The Bible also teaches that living water can also do the same for spiritual dehydration!*

John 7:37-38 "On the last day, that great day of the feast, Jesus stood and cried out, saying, 'If anyone thirsts, let him come to Me and drink. He who believes in Me, as the Scripture has said, out of his heart will flow rivers of living water.'" (NKJV)

BIG POPSICLE

So much ice has collected on the continent of Antarctica that if you cut it into sections one mile thick, you would end up with six million ice cubes. Should all of that ice melt, it would raise the sea level over the entire world by 260 feet! And not only that, the ice is so heavy that it has pushed the continent itself down several hundred feet.

ICEBERGS

On March 21, 2000, one of the largest icebergs ever documented broke free from the Antarctic's Ross Ice Shelf. A satellite image, taken 435 miles up, alerted scientists and mariners to the iceberg's birth. It was 183 miles long and 23 miles wide, with a surface area of 4,250 square miles.

But the biggest iceberg ever recorded was 208 miles long and 60 miles wide—a total of 12,000 square miles. That's larger than the country of Belgium! Even more amazing, it was spotted floating in the South Pacific. Icebergs wander far from their polar origins, reaching as far south as the island of Bermuda—a journey of 2,500 miles! One iceberg from the Antarctic reached almost as far north as Rio de Janeiro—a journey of 3,440 miles.

Now the tallest iceberg ever recorded was 550 feet—equaling a 50-story building. But remember that 10 percent of an iceberg's mass is above water, meaning the bulk of this titan could have reached 4,000 feet deep! *Jesus warned us that in the last days, lawlessness will abound because the love of many will grow cold. How can we have our hearts warmed and our first love rekindled in a spiritually cold world?*

Luke 11:9 *"And I say unto you, Ask, and it shall be given you; seek, and ye shall find; knock, and it shall be opened unto you."*

U.S. HISTORY AND CULTURE

Contents:

THEFT

The U.S. Commerce Department released some shocking figures. About four million people are caught shoplifting each year, but for every person caught it is estimated 35 go undetected.

If these estimates are accurate, it means that 140 million shoplifting incidents occur each year in a nation of nearly 300 million people. And according to another study, few shoplifters steal out of need: 70 percent of shoplifters are in the middle-income bracket; 20 percent had high incomes; and only 10 percent are considered poor.

Furthermore, according to insurance statistics, 30 percent of all business failures each year are a direct result of internal theft. Security officials estimate that 9 percent of all employees steal on a regular basis and 75 percent of those working in retail establishments steal to some degree, taking three times as much as shoplifters! And hotel managers count on 1 of every 3 guests stealing something.

The result of this plundering public is that prices everywhere skyrocket because of profit losses and increased security overhead.

John 10:9-11 "I am the door. If anyone enters by Me, he will be saved, and will go in and out and find pasture. The thief does not come except to steal, and to kill, and to destroy. I have come that they may have life, and that they may have it more abundantly. 'I am the good shepherd. The good shepherd gives His life for the sheep.'" (NKJV)

AND DID YOU KNOW...

- **Oh, Forget It!** There were 15 stripes on the official American flag before Congress passed a law setting the number to 13. The number had increased to 15 in 1795 to include Kentucky and Vermont. Since more and more states were joining the Union, the number of stripes was reduced to 13 as of July 4, 1818, to represent the original 13 states.

- **First-class Olives:** American Airlines saved $40,000 in 1987 by eliminating one olive from each salad served in first-class.

TAPS

You've probably heard the haunting song "Taps." That bugle melody creates tears in our eyes and lumps in our throats. Here's the story behind the song.

It began in 1862, following a Civil War battle near Harrison's Landing, Virginia. During the night, Union Captain Robert Ellicombe heard the moans of a soldier who lay severely wounded on the field. Not knowing if he was a Union or Confederate soldier, Captain Ellicombe decided to risk his life and bring the stricken man back for medical attention. Crawling on his stomach through gunfire, the Captain reached the wounded soldier and began pulling him toward his encampment. When the Captain finally reached his own lines, he discovered it was a Confederate soldier. But the soldier was dead. The Captain lit a lantern. He went numb with shock.

In the dim light, he recognized the young soldier as his own son. The boy had been studying music in the south when war broke out. Without telling his father, the boy had enlisted in the Confederate Army.

The following morning, the heartbroken father asked his superiors for permission to give his son a military burial. His request for a group of Army band members was only partially granted since his son was a Confederate soldier. Out of respect, they offered one musician.

The Captain chose a bugler, whom he asked to play a series of musical notes he had found on some paper in the pocket of his dead son's uniform. Later, bugler Oliver Wilcox Norton played the melody for Union General Daniel Adams Butterfield.

Soon the haunting melody, now known as "Taps," was used at all military funerals. Here are the words that went with the familiar music Captain Ellicombe found in his dead son's pocket:

"Day is done, Gone the sun, From the lakes, From the hills,
From the sky. All is well, safely rest. God is nigh.
Fading light, Dims the sight, And a star, Gems the sky,
Gleaming bright. From afar, Drawing nigh, Falls the night.
Thanks and praise, For our days, Neath the sun, Neath the stars,
Neath the sky, As we go, This we know, God is nigh."

This simple but enchanting song is also played on U.S. military bases around the world to mark the end of each day and time for sleep. *Did you know that the Bible teaches that death for the Christian is really only a brief sleep?*

AND DID YOU KNOW...

- **Hello, Dad:** There are more collect calls on this day than any other day of the year: Father's Day

- **Patient Fortitude:** The names of the two stone lions in front of the New York Public Library are Patience and Fortitude. They were named by then-mayor Fiorello LaGuardia.

- **Golf Mania:** Americans spend more than $630 million a year on golf balls.

THANKSGIVING

The U.S. day of thanks might not be celebrated today were it not for a remarkable woman named Sarah Hale (1788–1879).

It is well-known that pilgrims celebrated the first Thanksgiving Day in 1621 to give thanks for their bountiful harvest in the New World.

In 1789, President George Washington issued a Thanksgiving Day Proclamation to commemorate the first Pilgrim celebration. But Thomas Jefferson, the third president, discontinued it federally. After this, Thanksgiving was observed by some individual states on whatever date suited them.

Then in 1828, Mrs. Hale, a patient, persistent 34-year-old widow and mother of four, began campaigning for the restoration of Thanksgiving as a national holiday. For years she wrote letters and sought appointments with national leaders—from five different Presidents on down. Time after time she was politely rebuffed, sometimes being told it was "impractical," and "impossible." Other times she was chased off and scolded with "this-is-none-of-your-business!"

But Sarah was relentless. And in 1863, President Lincoln listened seriously to her plea that North and South "lay aside enmities and strife on (Thanksgiving) Day." He proclaimed the fourth Thursday of November to be the official "National Thanksgiving Day." This day was finally ratified by U.S. Congress in 1941.

Sarah Hale was the first woman magazine editor in the U.S. and the first person to use the word "lingerie" to describe undergarments. Sarah also helped start the first college for girls in the States, was also the first to suggest public playgrounds, and started the first day nursery for working mothers. But Sarah Hale is probably best remembered as author of the poem "Mary Had a Little Lamb."

AND DID YOU KNOW...

- **Missing Q:** The only letter not used in the spelling of any of the 50 states in America is Q.
- **No Rhyme, No Service:** No other words in the English language rhyme with the words month, orange, silver or purple.
- **One Is the Longest Number:** The longest one-syllable word in the English language is "screeched."

PONY EXPRESS

This thrilling part of American history transported mail 1,900 miles from St. Joseph, Missouri, to Sacramento, California, in only 10 days! Forty men, each riding 50 miles a day, dashed along the trail on 500 of the best horses the West could provide. Even though the express route was extremely hazardous, only one mail delivery was ever lost.

The Express is credited with helping to keep California in the Union by providing rapid communication between the two coasts.

News of Abraham Lincoln's election in 1860 and the outbreak of Civil War a year later reached California via the Pony Express.

Stringent rules were followed to conserve weight. Clothing was light, saddles were small and thin, and no weapons were carried. Even the horses wore light shoes or none at all! The mail pouches were also small, and letters had to be written on thin paper. Postage was $5.00 an ounce—a tremendous sum those days.

Yet despite all the scrupulous weight precautions, each rider carried a full-sized Bible! It was presented when a rider joined the unit, and he took it with him on his routes. Many are surprised to learn that among the Bible-toting couriers in the Pony Express was a young man named William Cody, later known as Buffalo Bill.

Sadly, after only a year-and-a-half of operation, the service was discontinued when the Pacific Telegraph Company completed its line to San Francisco.

Today, international communications travel at the speed of light—but for thousands of years God has been sending messages to man at the speed of thought.

THE STATUE OF LIBERTY

This most honored symbol in America arrived after 20 years of dedication and at a cost of more than $4 million. French sculptor Frederic Bartholdi was inspired to build the enormous monument after seeing the colossi in Egypt. After examining candidates, he chose his mother as the statue's model.

The statue was built in France, then dismantled and packaged into 200 massive crates for transport to New York. A French warship transported the gift across the Atlantic. On the way, a terrible storm threatened to sink the vessel. The crew begged the captain to dump the heavy crates into the sea to lighten the load, but the captain responded, "This ship will sink before I give up liberty."

Real liberty requires dedication, self control and sacrifice. But the devil has a counterfeit for every truth of God, including liberty.

Romans 8:38-39 "For I am persuaded, that neither death, nor life, nor angels, nor principalities, nor powers, nor things present, nor things to come, Nor height, nor depth, nor any other creature, shall be able to separate us from the love of God, which is in Christ Jesus our Lord."

BARBERSHOPS

Do you know why barbershops have a red, blue and white spiral out front? It's not from patriotic roots.

During the Middle Ages, dentistry in Europe was practiced by "barber-surgeons." These community professionals served the townspeople by performing a wide variety of services, which ranged from cutting hair, extracting teeth, and bloodletting.

For hundreds of years, physicians would bleed people with fevers believing they had too much blood. Sometimes light bleeding was accomplished by applying leaches!. For more intense bleeding, the patient would hold the top of a ceramic pillar with their hand while the physician made an incision in the wrist allowing the blood to drain down the pillar where they measured it in a basin. Physicians would examine the blood color and quality as it ran spiraling down the pole into the basin. The reason for the two colors on the pole is because veins are generally blue and arteries red. Gradually, dentistry and surgery were taken over by specialist and the barber was left with his scissors and comb. But the spiral pole still endures. It makes us shutter to think that people once believed blood letting would bring healing.

1 Peter 1:18-21 "Forasmuch as ye know that ye were not redeemed with corruptible things, as silver and gold, from your vain conversation received by tradition from your fathers; But with the precious blood of Christ, as of a lamb without blemish and without spot: Who verily was foreordained before the foundation of the world, but was manifest in these last times for you, Who by him do believe in God, that raised him up from the dead, and gave him glory; that your faith and hope might be in God."

AND DID YOU KNOW...

- **Dreamy:** "Dreamt" is the only English word that ends in the letters "mt".

- **State Names:** Until 1796, there was a state in the United States called Franklin. Today it's known as Tennessee!

- **Bad Word:** The word "highjack" originated during prohibition. When a truck of illegal liquor was taken, the gunman would say "HIGH, JACK," indicating how the driver should raise his hands.

GAMBLING

In 1998, U.S. citizens lost $60 billion in legal gambling. That figure has increased every year for more than two decades, often at double-digit rates—and there is no end in sight!

The most amazing fact is that over the past 25 years, the United States has been transformed from a nation in which legalized gambling was rare and limited into one in which such activity is common and growing. Today, all but two states have some form of legalized gambling. Lotteries have been established in 37 states and the District of Columbia, with more states poised to follow. Indian casinos operate in every region of the country. From cruise ships to riverboats, gambling sites continue to proliferate.

Internet and telephone gambling is legalized in more states, so an increasingly large percentage of the public can now place a bet without ever leaving home! Universally available, "round-the-clock" gambling may soon be a reality.

The problem is that gambling now accounts for a significant portion of a state's income, so who wants to kill the goose that lays the golden eggs?

AND DID YOU KNOW...

- **Statue Statutes:** If a statue of a person on a horse has both front legs in the air, the person died in battle; if the horse has one front leg in the air, the person died as a result of wounds received in battle; if the horse has all four legs on the ground, the person died of natural causes.

- **Short and Sweet:** "I am," is the shortest complete sentence in the English language.

- **Rare A:** If you were to spell out numbers, you'd have to go to one thousand before you got to the letter A.

DAM BREAK!

At midnight, March 12, 1928, one of the worst catastrophes in California history occurred: the St. Francis Dam broke.

Huge torrents of water washed down the San Francisquito

Canyon, killing hundreds in its path. The official body count is 450 dead, but the actual number was substantially higher, since San Francisquito Canyon was home to hundreds of transient farm workers that were never counted. This would bring the death toll to higher than the famous 1906 San Francisco earthquake.

The dam broke just under two years after its completion. More than 900 buildings and $13 million in property were destroyed in the flood. But the greatest tragedy of this disaster was that no one needed to perish!

There was ample warning time on the morning it broke. A worker at the dam saw water leaking through the dam wall. He warned his boss, William Mulholland, about this danger. After looking at the dam, Mulholland, who also designed the structure, decided that there was no cause for concern. But that night, the dam broke, sending a wall of water as high as 140 feet down the canyon through Saugus, Fillmore, Santa Paula and finally the Pacific Ocean. It traveled 54 miles in 5.5 hours, destroying everything in its path.

The wall of standards that separates the church from the world has more than a little seepage ... there is a major breach about to hemorrhage.

AMERICAN FLAG

The U.S. flag is a respected symbol of this nation's freedom—and rightly so. USFlag.org provides the following standards of flag etiquette, among others: It must never be dipped to any person; should not be used merely as decoration or advertising; should not be marked on or embroidered onto any temporary item. It is not to be part of a costume or athletic uniform. It must never be used as a receptacle for holding anything. It should remain clean and no part should touch the ground or any other object when lowered. It should be received with open arms and folded neatly and ceremoniously. *How much more so should we treat God's Word?*

Psalm 119:11 "Thy word have I hid in mine heart, that I might not sin against thee."

Psalm 119:103 "How sweet are thy words unto my taste! yea, sweeter than honey to my mouth."

AGAINST THE LAW

Did you know it is against the law to:
- Doze off under a hair dryer in Florida?
- Play hopscotch on Sunday in Missouri?
- Hunt Camels in Arizona?
- Insert a penny in your ear in Hawaii?
- Transport an ice cream cone in your pocket in Kentucky?
- Tie a giraffe to a telephone pole in Atlanta?
- Catch mice without a license in Cleveland?
- Whistle underwater in Vermont?
- Put a skunk in your boss' desk in Michigan?
- Bathe less then once a year in Kentucky?
- Detonate a nuclear weapon within Chico, California, city limits (which carries a punishment of $500)?
- To pawn your dentures in Las Vegas?
- To burp or sneeze in a certain church in Omaha, Nebraska?
- To throw knives at men wearing striped suits in Natoma, Kansas?

There are about two million laws in the United States. If a person could review them at the rate of two a day, he could be qualified to act as a law-abiding citizen in about 6,000 years.

Yet any child can learn that God was able to summarize the whole duty of man toward God and his neighbor in 10 simple principles. How sad it is that many pastors teaching the 10 Commandments concern themselves with too many other laws.

Matthew 22:37-40 "Jesus said unto him, THOU SHALT LOVE THE LORD THY GOD WITH ALL THY HEART, AND WITH ALL THY SOUL, AND WITH ALL THY MIND. This is the first and great commandment. And the second is like unto it, THOU SHALT LOVE THY NEIGHBOR AS THYSELF. On these two commandments hang all the law and the prophets."

ALCOHOL IN U.S. HISTORY

Two fatal drinks changed history. On the last day of Lincoln's life, the great emancipator said: "We have cleared up a colossal job. Slavery is abolished. After reconstruction, the next great question will be the overthrow and suppression of the legalized liquor traffic."

That evening, John Wilkes Booth stopped in a saloon to fill himself with liquor to nerve himself for his evil plan. That same night, Lincoln's bodyguard left the theater for a drink of liquor at the same saloon! While he was away, Booth shot Lincoln. These two drinks were among the most costly in American history.

Luke 21:34-36 "And take heed to yourselves, lest at any time your hearts be overcharged with surfeiting, and drunkenness, and cares of this life, and so that day come upon you unawares. For as a snare shall it come on all them that dwell on the face of the whole earth. Watch ye therefore, and pray always, that ye may be accounted worthy to escape all these things ... "

DEBT-FREE NATION

In 1837, President Andrew Jackson erased all but $37,513 of Washington's red ink. In his inaugural address, he said, "Under every aspect ... considered it would appear that advantage must result from the observance of a strict and faithful economy. This I shall aim ... [to] facilitate the extinguishment of the national debt, the unnecessary duration of which is incompatible with real independence, and because it will counteract that tendency to public and private profligacy."

ANTACID NATION

One of the best-selling over-the-counter remedies in North America is antacids—eaten like candy by millions feeling too anxious. In fact, we spend nearly $2 billion each year fighting stomach ailments often related to stress. Ironically, regular use of antacids might have a debilitating effect on the human body: It's been linked to esophagus erosion, diarrhea, constipation, and a host of other digestion problems—along with preventing protein absorption and disrupting other medicines' effectiveness. Like most drugs, antacids really only treat the symptoms of what's really going wrong inside us. *A better diet, exercise, a thorough check-up and most important, trust in God may be the ultimate steps in ridding oneself of this dangerous pill-popping problem.*

John 14:27 "Peace I leave with you, my peace I give unto you: not as the world giveth, give I unto you. Let not your heart be troubled, neither let it be afraid."

DECORATION DAY

May 30, 1868, marked the first Decoration Day, designated as a time of remembrance for Americans who died in their nation's defense during the Civil War. Later, this date became known as Memorial Day and was expanded to include all service men and women who fought and died for the United States in war. Nearly 1.5 million Americans have died in wartime service, fighting to bring peace and stability for their homeland. Of course, no human war has ever provided lasting peace—since the signing of the World War I Armistice in 1918, for every year of war, there have been just two minutes of political peace. *However, the Bible tells us that at the conclusion of the greatest war ever fought, humanity will know true peace forever.*

John 16:33 "These things I have spoken unto you, that in me ye might have peace. In the world ye shall have tribulation: but be of good cheer; I have overcome the world."

DOGGED LOGO

Everyone is familiar with the RCA logo with Nipper the dog listening to the RCA grammaphone. But the original picture had both the dog and the grammaphone sitting on his dead master's casket. The idea being that the closest thing to his dead master's voice was the RCA grammaphone. The ad was eventually considered too morbid and they removed the casket.

DEBTOR'S PRISON

In the nineteenth century, being thrown in jail for debt was common practice in the United States and England. Unfortunately, the jailed not only had to pay back their debt, they also had to pay for the imprisonment! Many debtors died while serving time, unable to work or find funds to get out.

The Annapolis jail, were many debtors were holed, was described as "a place of death and torments to many unfortunate people." It was also said to be "so filthy and nasty that it is exceedingly nauseating." Some prisoners were held under these conditions for debts as small as 50 cents!

One of our countries most important citizens, a signer of the Declaration of Independence, landed in debtors' prison. Robert Morris (1733–1806) was one of the nation's Founding Fathers and even helped finance the American Revolution. In late 1776, George Washington called upon Morris to raise cash to fight the British. Washington had thousands of troops without clothing, food, guns, or ammunition—and there was no treasury to turn to for help. So Morris loaned $10,000 of his money to the government, which used the cash to provision the desperate troops at Valley Forge. Those soldiers went on to win the Battle of Trenton, which changed the course of the war. Morris emptied his own pockets and borrowed against his assets and property to allow Washington to continue to fight the war. He also helped in negotiating loans from France.

Indeed, Robert Morris became the chief financier of the American Revolution and, in 1781, was appointed by Congress as the first superintendent of finance. Sadly, because of some bad land investments, he was arrested for debt in 1798 and confined to prison in Philadelphia, until liberated by the passage of the national bankruptcy law in 1802.

It's hard to believe a man who lent money to George Washington to fight the Revolutionary War would later be cast into a debtors' prison by the country he helped to liberate. *But more amazingly, Jesus tells a parable of a man who did something similar to his own friend.*

WORLD HISTORY AND CULTURE

Contents:

DRIVING SOUTHPAW

Have you ever wondered why some countries have traffic moving on the right side of the road while others have people driving on the left side—such as the United Kingdom? The theory says that in yonder days, nobility rode their horses on the left so that their sword hand, usually the right, would be on the same side as an oncoming horseman. Naturally, it made sense for peasants to walk on the right, facing the oncoming traffic of armed nobility. This is how most of Europe practiced road etiquette for many years.

However, during the French revolution, many aristocrats were executed—and even after the revolution, it was poor luck to be mistaken as nobility. So the citizens of France began riding on the right side. Then came Napoleon, who carried this practice with him as he conquered large parts of Europe. Along the way, he built the first international road system since the Romans. But Napoleon's defeat at Waterloo kept him from making it to England. Therefore, that island and its territories continued riding on the left.

Today the words "right" and "left" have also come to represent opposite extremes in politics and religion. *Did you know that the Bible teaches these extremes will come together in the last days to worship the beast and its image?*

BIBLICALLY LONG-WINDED

A 46-year-old Anglican vicar from Lancashire, England, delivered a 28-hour, 45-minute sermon to establish a new world record for the longest unscripted speech. Chris Sterry began this marathon sermon June 29, 2001. While speaking, the former Old Testament professor was not allowed to repeat himself, talk nonsense, or pause for more than 10 seconds—though he was permitted a 15-minute break every eight hours. Sterry's sermon covered the first four books of the Bible and was broadcast live every 15 minutes on CNN throughout June 30. He undertook the challenge as a way of raising 2,000 pounds (£) for his church.

His biggest wish? "I hope that those who come to listen to it will get something out of it." Sadly, news reports do not indicate whether any of his parishioners also lasted the entire distance.

PITCAIRN PARADISE

You've probably heard about the Mutiny on the Bounty, but one part of the story that needs retelling is the transformation wrought by one incredible book. Nine mutineers, six Tahitian men, and twelve women put ashore on Pitcairn Island in 1790 after the mutiny. One of the sailors began distilling alcohol, and soon after the little colony was plunged into debauchery, vice, and murder.

Ten years later, only one of the men, John Adams, had survived, surrounded by 10 native women and a bushel of mixed children. One day, this sailor discovered a Bible in an old chest from the Bounty. He began reading it, and his life changed. He then started teaching it to the others, and as a result, the lives of all those on the island were dramatically transformed.

Discovered in 1808 by an American whaling ship, Pitcairn had become a prosperous community with no jail, whisky, crime, or laziness. Today, descendants of the original islanders still live there in a moralistic society on one of the most isolated islands in the world. *Can the Bible principles really transform a culture from vice and crime to tranquility today?*

James 3:17 "But the wisdom that is from above is first pure, then peaceable, gentle, and easy to be entreated, full of mercy and good fruits, without partiality, and without hypocrisy."

QUETZACOATL QUAGMIRE

In the fourteenth century, the Aztec empire was one of the most powerful and sophisticated civilizations in the Western Hemisphere. Yet this kingdom of 2 million was conquered within a year by a Spanish force of just 600 lightly armed men. How did it happen?

The Aztecs believed in the coming of Quetzalcoatl (kèt-säl´ko-ä-tal), a legendary feathered, bearded, and light-skinned god-king to return from across the sea to Mexico. It so happened that this coincided with the arrival of the conquistadors on Spanish galleons. In 1519, the conquistador leader Hernando Cortez impersonated this god of the Aztecs—astutely assuming the mantle of Quetzalcoatl to befuddle the superstitious king Montezuma. By fooling the native peoples, Cortez was able to complete the Spanish conquest, which included the enslaving and murder of the local tribe.

The vague and ambiguous prophecies of the Aztec god served as an awesome pretext for counterfeit. Jesus also foretold that in the last days there would be many false christs and false prophets who would deceive the majority of the world.

Matthew 24:11 "And many false prophets shall rise, and shall deceive many."

Matthew 24:24 "For there shall arise false Christs, and false prophets, and shall show great signs and wonders; insomuch that, if it were possible, they shall deceive the very elect."

AND DID YOU KNOW...

- **Law Poetry:** The French statesman Ferdinand Flocon succeeded in making a poem out of the law. He took the whole French Civil Code—with its 2,281 articles, statues, annotations, and amendments—and converted them into an immaculate poem of 120,000 words—perfect in rhyme and meter. He did it ostensibly to make the many laws more palatable. Someone once said the more lawless a people, the more laws they will need.

- **Union Jack:** The flag of the U.K. is properly known as the Union flag. It is only called the Union Jack when it is flown from the jack mast of a ship.

GLADIATORS

From the Latin *gladius*, which means "sword," gladiators were professional fighters who performed spectacles of armed combat in the amphitheaters of ancient Rome. The practice of armed slaves fighting to the death originated in central Italy and lasted for more than 700 years.

The first gladiator exhibition in Rome was in 264 B.C., when three pairs of gladiators fought as part of a funeral celebration. By 174 B.C., 37 pairs participated. On one occasion, Julius Caesar ordered large-scale exhibitions with 300 pairs of combatants! But the largest contest of gladiators was given by the Emperor Trajan as part of a victory celebration in A.D. 107 and included 5,000 pairs of fighters! It appears that as the years went by, each generation wanted something more horrific, violent and perverted to keep the masses entertained. Eventually, the Emperor Domitian presented combats between women and between dwarfs.

Gladiators were typically male slaves, condemned criminals, prisoners of war, and sometimes Christians. Forced to become swordsmen, they were trained in schools called ludi, and special measures were taken to discipline them and prevent suicides. Occasionally, freedmen and Roman citizens entered the arena, as did the insane Emperor Commodus. The escaped gladiator Spartacus avenged his captivity by leading an army of slaves in an insurrection that terrorized southern Italy from 73 to 71 B.C.

According to tradition, an overpowered opponent's fate was left to the spectators. If they wished to spare the defeated man, they waved their handkerchiefs, but they turned down their thumbs when they wished him dead. A successful gladiator received great acclaim—poets praised him, gems and vases held his likeness, and ladies of nobility pampered him. A gladiator who survived many combats might even be relieved from further obligation.

Gladiators were divided into various light- and heavy-armored classes. Some fought with a net and a trident, some with different weapons, and from horseback or chariots. Although Constantine the Great denounced gladiatorial contests in A.D. 325, they continued to be held until about A.D. 500 when Rome fell.

Sir Edward Gibbon wrote in his classic *The History of the Decline and Fall of the Roman Empire* that the mad craze for pleasure and sports become more brutal each year and is one of the five reasons the empire fell. *Is it possible that the world today is following the same yearning for carnal entertainment that led to the fall of ancient Rome?*

AND DID YOU KNOW...

- **Poker Blitz:** In Australia, the state of New South Wales has more than 10 per cent of the poker machines in the whole world. It is not uncommon to see housewives playing the slot machine while shelling peas after their mid-morning shopping.

- **Law School Nightmare:** All the laws of ancient Rome were ordered by Emperor Justinian to be compiled during the 6th century. With 16 assistants, Tribonian came up with 2,000 volumes after three years.

HONEYMOON

The accepted practice of Babylon weddings of 4,000 years ago was that for a month after the nuptials, the bride's father supplied his son-in-law with all the mead he could drink. Mead is a honey beer, and because their calendar was lunar based, this period was called the "honey month"—or what we know today as the "honeymoon."

PASS THE ALKA SELTZER

The largest single dish served in the world is roasted camel. It's true! To celebrate a wedding or honor a visiting dignitary, Mohammedan tribes in the Arabian, Syrian, and North African deserts usually give a feast where the main dish is without equal in size.

This is how the stuffed camel is put together: Eggs are stuffed inside fish; fish are in turn stuffed into chickens; the chickens are then stuffed into sheep, which are roasted. Then the entire cooked sheep are stuffed into a camel. This colossal culinary concoction is the main course at these special feasts. Would you like fries with that?

Jesus accused the religious leaders of his day as "blind guides, which strain at a gnat, and swallow a camel." Sadly, many Christians have been swallowing a popular lie that teaches "As long as you pray over your food God does not care what you eat or drink." But what does the Bible really say?

TROJAN HORSE

Legend has it that when the Greeks were unable to capture the city of Troy, even after a 10-year siege, they finally resorted to this clever stratagem. The Greek army pretended to sail away and left on the shore a huge, hollow wooden horse as an apparent victory gift. However, the gift was actually filled with several armed warriors! Sinon, a Greek spy inside Troy, persuaded the Trojans to bring the horse within the city walls, saying that to do so would mysteriously make Troy invincible. That night, Sinon released the troops hiding in the gigantic horse. After killing the Trojan guards, they opened the gates to the waiting Greek soldiers, and Troy was captured and burned.

Matthew 7:15 "Beware of false prophets, which come to you in sheep's clothing, but inwardly they are ravening wolves."

HUMAN GODS?

In the spring of 331, after conquering the Persians and Egyptians, Alexander the Great made a pilgrimage to the great temple and oracle of Amon-Ra—the Egyptian god of the sun, whom the Greeks identified as Zeus.

The early Egyptian pharaohs were believed to be sons of Amon-Ra; Alexander, the new ruler of Egypt, wanted the god to acknowledge him as his son. The pilgrimage apparently was successful, and it might have confirmed in the young king's belief that he was divine. Just before he died, Alexander ordered the Greek cities to worship him as a god. The order was largely nullified shortly after he issued it by his death. I wonder if there's a connection?

Captain James Cook sailed around the world and managed to survive a thousand perils. But when he landed on the island paradise of Hawaii, the primitive natives took him for a god. He allowed the Hawaiians to view him as divine and worship him. When on his return voyage, they found out he was not a God—they then killed and mutilated the renowned captain.

AND DID YOU KNOW...

- **Topsy-Turvy Year:** 1961 was the most recent year that could be written both upside-down and right side-up. The next year will be 6009!

- **Letters to Avoid:** Certain sounds in the English language are real germ spreaders, particularly the sounds of f, p, t, d, and s.

- **A.D./B.C.:** The abbreviation A.D. (Anno Domini, "Year of Our Lord") should be placed in front of the year—thus, you get 417 B.C. but A.D. 2000.

JUBILEE

Many Americans would be uncommonly thrilled if the United States practiced the Jewish Jubilee. Every 50 years, initiated by a blast through a ram's horn, Jews would forgive each other of financial debts and set their slaves free. The Jubilee was established as a reminder that the Jewish people were set free from their constant mistakes and bad habits. Unfortunately, with the destruction of the temple and the scattering of the Jewish people, the Jubilee is no longer celebrated.

THE DARK CONTINENT

When the European colonial powers embarked on conquering Africa, they labeled it "The Dark Continent." They saw it as a vast and dangerous place full of savage people. This could not have been further from the truth, as Africa and her multi-hued people have spawned some of the world's most advanced, colorful and exotic civilizations—it is well established that African cultures were among the earliest to employ iron, build cities and develop trade routes. However, in the 7th century, Islam replaced Christianity as the dominant religion, steeping the continent into a Christ-less darkness.

Luke 1:76-79 *"And thou, child, shalt be called the prophet of the Highest: for thou shalt go before the face of the Lord to prepare his ways; To give knowledge of salvation unto his people by the remission of their sins, Through the tender mercy of our God; whereby the dayspring from on high hath visited us, To give light to them that sit in darkness and in the shadow of death, to guide our feet into the way of peace."*

PUZZLING FACTS

In the 1760s, European mapmakers pasted maps onto wood and cut them into pieces. The "dissected map" has been a successful geography toy for children all over the world. But perhaps the biggest surprise is how adults have been captured by the urge to connect! Jigsaw puzzles for adults emerged around 1900 and soon became all the rage. Early puzzle pieces did not interlock, so a cough could ruin an evening, and most puzzles came without a picture to guide them by. *Today, we spend millions of dollar trying to find those missing pieces, but the Bible provides the ultimate missing piece to all of life's puzzling scenarios.*

Romans 8:32 *"He that spared not his own Son, but delivered him up for us all, how shall he not with him also freely give us all things?"*

KRAKATOA

One of the loudest sounds in world history was the terrific volcanic explosion of Krakatoa in Indonesia in 1883. The blast's power was equivalent to about 100 megatons of dynamite and could be heard more than 3,000 miles away! In fact, the sound could be heard by the human ear over 1/10th of the earth's surface.

More than 36,000 people were killed, and 165 coastal villages were destroyed—mostly by the giant sea waves that reached heights of 120 feet. The deadly waves roared at 316 mph, devastating everything in their path and hurling coral blocks ashore that weighed as much as 600 tons while traveling a distance of 3,800 nautical miles in 12 hours. In addition, the tremendous explosion blew five cubic miles of debris into the atmosphere. The debris settled over an area of 300,000 square miles.

The massive dust cloud blocked out sunlight, plunging Jakarta (100 miles away) into complete darkness. For more than three years, the residual produced some of the most beautiful, unusual, and brilliant-red sunsets the world has witnessed. Three months after the eruption, the vivid flaming sunsets were so intense that fire engines were often called out in New York and New England to quench imaginary infernos.

Thirteen days after the initial blast, fine ash and aerosol, 30 miles up in the stratosphere, had circled the equator. The volcanic dust veil created such spectacular atmospheric effects as blue and green suns and also acted as a solar radiation filter, lowering global temperatures as much as two degrees. Temperatures did not return to normal for five years.

The eruption of Krakatoa was one of the loudest, most powerful and visible events in modern times. Did you know that the book of Revelation also pictures brilliant and powerful angels in the heavens proclaiming a loud message of warning and hope just prior to Jesus' return?

Revelation 8:13 "*And I beheld, and heard an angel flying through the midst of heaven, saying with a loud voice, Woe, woe, woe, to the inhabiters of the earth by reason of the other voices of the trumpet of the three angels, which are yet to sound!*"

Contents:

> The Frozen Ship ● The Shark's Papers ● Message in a Bottle
> ● No 911 Service ● Not-So Nursery Rhyme ● A Century Ago

THE FROZEN SHIP

The Frozen Ship: A vessel discovered among the icebergs of the Arctic Ocean still had its captain aboard, frozen resting over his logbook. The crew was discovered, some in their hammocks and some in the cabin, also all frozen to death. The last date in the logbook showed that for 13 years, the ship had been moving among the icebergs, "a drifting sepulchre, manned by a frozen crew." *Are there not churches in a like condition?*

Revelation 3:1-2 "And unto the angel of the church in Sardis write; These things saith he that hath the seven Spirits of God, and the seven stars; I know thy works, that thou hast a name that thou livest, and art dead. Be watchful, and strengthen the things which remain, that are ready to die: for I have not found thy works perfect before God."

THE SHARK'S PAPERS

In 1799, the American sailing vessel Nancy was seized by the British and taken into Port Royal, Jamaica, under suspicion of carrying contraband. Before the Nancy was boarded, the captain had the crew throw the forbidden

freight and the ship's cargo papers into the sea. At the trial, the captain and officers were about to be acquitted for lack of evidence, when the captain of another ship walked into the court with the Nancy's original cargo papers. His men discovered them in the stomach of a shark they harpooned that morning. Consequently, the defendants were convicted. Today, these remarkable documents, called "The Shark's Papers," are on exhibit in Kingston, Jamaica.

AND DID YOU KNOW...

- **Sugar Free UPC:** The first product to have a UPC bar code on its packaging was Wrigley's gum.

- **Typists' Nightmare:** Skepticisms is the longest word that alternates hands when typing.

- **The Real Alphabet:** The letters of the alphabet in order of their frequency of use are: ETAISONHRDLUCM-FWYPGVBKJQXZ

- **Fly Facts:** Pope Adrian VI choked to death after a fly got stuck in his throat as he was drinking from a water fountain. Other fly facts: Contrary to popular myth, flies do exist in Alaska. They act as worms, which are not present there. Flies, like butterflies, taste with their feet. And a fly always jumps backwards for a quick getaway when you try to hit it. Amazingly, if all the offspring survived, 190,000,000,000,000,000,000 flies could be produced in four months by the offspring of a single pair of flies.

MESSAGE IN A BOTTLE

In 1493, while in the West Indies, Christopher Columbus tossed a bottle overboard that contained a message for Queen Isabella I of Spain. In 1852, 359 years later, the bottle was found by the captain of an American ship and delivered to Queen Isabella II of Spain. And in 1956, a bottle was washed up on the north coast of Jamaica containing a faded message dated 1750. The writer wrote that his ship was on fire and sinking.

NO 911 SERVICE

In 1928 John Flynn, a Presbyterian minister, helped to establish a "Flying Doctor Base" to serve the remote people of the Australian outback. The desperate need for this service was made clear when Flynn heard about a ranch hand with a spear embedded in his chest. The man had to be carried in a hammock slung between two horses 400 miles to a station where he waited two weeks for a train that carried him 600 miles to a hospital in Adelaide.

Matthew 4:23 "And Jesus went about all Galilee, teaching in their synagogues, and preaching the gospel of the kingdom, and healing all manner of sickness and all manner of disease among the people."

NOT-SO NURSERY RHYME

"Ring Around the Rosy" is about the plague. Infected people would get red circular sores ("ring around the rosy"), which would smell very badly so people would put flowers on their bodies to cover the smell of the sores ("a pocket full of posies"). Then those who died from the plague would be burned to reduce the spread of the disease ("ashes, ashes, we all fall down!")

Revelation 22:3-5 "And there shall be no more curse: but the throne of God and of the Lamb shall be in it; and his servants shall serve him: And they shall see his face; and his name shall be in their foreheads. And there shall be no night there; and they need no candle, neither light of the sun; for the Lord God giveth them light: and they shall reign for ever and ever."

A CENTURY AGO

- The average life expectancy in the United States was 47.
- Only 14 percent of the homes in the United States had a bathtub.
- Only 8 percent of homes had a phone. A 3-minute call from Denver to New York City cost 11 dollars
- There were only 8,000 cars in the nation and only 144 miles of paved roads.
- The maximum speed limit in most cities was 10 mph.

- Alabama, Mississippi, Iowa, and Tennessee were each more heavily populated than California. With a mere 1.4 million residents, California was only the 21st most populous state in the Union.
- The tallest structure in the world was the Eiffel Tower.
- The average wage in America was 22 cents an hour. The average worker made between $200 and $400 per year. A competent accountant could expect to earn $2,000 per year, a dentist $2,500 per year, a veterinarian up to $4,000 per year, and a mechanical engineer about $5,000.
- More than 95 percent of all births in the United States took place at home.
- 90 percent of all U.S. physicians had no college education. Instead, they attended medical schools, many of which were condemned in the press and by the government as "substandard."
- Sugar cost 4 cents a pound. Eggs were 14 cents a dozen. Coffee cost 15 cents a pound.
- Most women only washed their hair once a month and used borax or egg yolks for shampoo.
- Canada passed a law prohibiting poor people from entering the country for any reason, either as travelers or immigrants.
- The five leading causes of death in the U.S. were:
    1. Pneumonia and influenza
    2. Tuberculosis
    3. Diarrhea
    4. Heart disease
    5. Stroke
- The American flag had 45 stars. Arizona, Oklahoma, New Mexico, Hawaii and Alaska hadn't been admitted to the Union yet.
- "Ride-by-shootings," in which teenage boys galloped down the street on horses and started randomly shooting at houses, carriages, or anything else that caught their fancy, were an ongoing problem in Denver and other cities in the West.
- The population of Las Vegas, Nevada was 30. The remote desert community was inhabited by only a handful of ranchers and their families.
- Plutonium, insulin, and antibiotics hadn't been discovered yet.
- Scotch tape, crossword puzzles, and iced tea hadn't been invented.
- There was no Mother's Day or Father's Day.
- 1 in 10 U.S. adults couldn't read or write. Only 6 percent of all Americans had graduated from high school.

- Marijuana, heroin, and morphine were all available over the counter at corner drugstores. According to one pharmacist, "Heroin clears the complexion, gives buoyancy to the mind, regulates the stomach and the bowels, and is, in fact, a perfect guardian of health."
- Punch card data processing had recently been developed, and early predecessors of the modern computer were used for the first time by the government to help compile the 1900 census.
- 18 percent of households in the United States had at least one full-time servant or domestic.
- There were about 230 reported murders in the U.S. annually.

AMAZING FACTS

Visit us online at
www.amazingfacts.org
and check out our online catalog
filled with other great books, videos,
CDs, audiotapes, and more!

Don't miss our FREE online
Bible Prophecy course at
www.bibleuniverse.com
Enroll today and
expand your universe!